Equal opportunities for women and men
European Community acts

Employment & social affairs

Equality between women and men

European Commission
Directorate-General for Employment, Industrial Relations
and Social Affairs
Unit V/D.5

Manuscript completed in June 1998

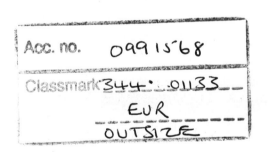
A great deal of additional information on the European Union is available on the Internet.
It can be accessed through the Europa server (http://europa.eu.int).

Cataloguing data can be found at the end of this publication.

Luxembourg: Office for Official Publications of the European Communities, 1999

ISBN 92-827-7665-4

Printed in Germany

PRINTED ON WHITE CHLORINE-FREE PAPER

Foreword

Equal treatment for men and women is integral to the European Community's social policy. It is crucial both to its economic success and its social cohesion in the future.

The principle of equal treatment has developed from the isolated provision of equal pay for equal work contained in Article 119 of the Treaty, to a fully fledged programme of equality measures. Since the early 1970s the Commission has been a driving force, whether through its proposals for directives, awareness-raising campaigns or funding initiatives, in putting the need for equality under the spotlight, bringing home its importance to the key players, and working in partnership with them to meet this need. By key players, we mean not only the Member States, but also regional and local authorities, the two sides of industry, company managers, academia, the media and the citizens of Europe themselves.

Significant progress has been accomplished in terms of secondary legislation: several directives have laid the legal groundwork for radical changes in attitudes and practices. Through its case-law, the Court of Justice has helped to clarify and extend the concept of equal opportunities, as regards access to employment, and social security and pay. In addition, the Recommendations, Resolutions and Communications of both Council and Commission have reinforced this focus by providing a wealth of guidelines on good practice and setting out a framework for future action.

With the advent of the Treaty of Maastricht, an additional procedure for adopting legislation was introduced, in the guise of the Social Policy Agreement. Given the Commission's emphasis on the importance of partnership to equal opportunities, it is, therefore, perhaps no accident that the first text to be agreed by the Social Partners, and translated into European law under the Social Policy Agreement, related to equality (in particular to parental leave). The Treaty of Amsterdam has also reinforced the importance of equal opportunities and has opened up some new ground (Articles 2, 3, 13 and 141). Equality between men and women will be amongst the express objectives of the Community and now has a specific legal base.

The legal texts found in this supplement provide the backbone for Community policy on equal opportunities. However, it takes more than just directives to promote *de facto* equality. Legislation must not only be sound on paper — it must be effective in practice. Too often, citizens are not aware of the rights conferred on them by Community law, or find it difficult to access the mechanisms which enforce these rights. It is with this in mind that a major priority of the Community's Action Programme on Equal Opportunities is to stimulate increased participation by all relevant legal practitioners in this area, to improve procedures for enforcement of Community law, and increase the quality and quantity of information on European law and social policies.

We know that, even with all the legislation in place, there is still much work to do and we will continue to step up and expand our efforts in this field if the European Community is to address the inequalities which persist. The status of women in the labour market provides a prime example of continuing inequality: the rate of unemployment amongst women is still higher than amongst men; women account for the majority of the long-term unemployed, they often have low-skilled, poorly-paid and insecure jobs, and there are still gaps in pay between men and women in all regions of the Union.

In response to these challenges, in addition to its legislative programme, the Commission has brought forward a series of multi-annual action programmes — programmes which set out a framework within which to develop policy to meet specific needs, and which provide funding and support for innovative transnational measures in the field of equality.

Real equality can only be achieved if we as a Community make equal opportunities *everybody's* priority — a priority within every field of policy, and at every level of activity, whether at European, national, or local level. The integration of this 'equality reflex' into every sphere of policy at every level is known as 'mainstreaming'. The mainstreaming principle is one which will set the tone for implementing our Fourth Programme and one which I am actively pursuing with my colleagues in the Commission. Our aim is to ensure that equal opportunities are built into all policies and become a common strand of Community action. This is why the Commission services are currently reviewing all of the policies and actions of the Commission in which equal opportunities do, or could, play a role. This work will form the basis for us to bring forward new ideas on how to integrate women's concerns into broader areas of policy.

It is this combination of legislation, mainstreaming and practical initiatives which will support a flourishing and competitive European Union, and will enable it to use the talents of both men and women to their full potential. Equality is the key to building a society which values the contribution of women equally with men — and which respects the needs of both to balance work and family commitments. It promotes a culture which respects the dignity of women and men, and which looks equally to both for leadership in decision-making.

The ultimate goal of the European Community must be that the boys and girls of the next century will not see their futures limited by their gender — but will have the full range of opportunities in both education and employment open to them, without hindrance or prejudice.

Pádraig Flynn
Member of the European Commission
Responsible for Employment and Social Affairs

Contents

Council decision

Commission decisions

Council recommendations

Commission recommendations

Council resolutions

Council conclusions

Commission communications

Treaty

Treaty of Amsterdam amending the Treaties establishing the European Communities, signed at Amsterdam, 2 October 1997

Article 2

The Community shall have as its task, by establishing a common market and an economic and monetary union and by implementing common policies or activities referred to in Articles 3 and 4, to promote throughout the Community a harmonious, balanced and sustainable development of economic activities, a high level of employment and of social protection, equality between men and women, sustainable and non-inflationary growth, a high degree of competitiveness and convergence of economic performance, a high level of protection and improvement of the quality of the environment, the raising of the standard of living and quality of life, and economic and social cohesion and solidarity among Member States.

Article 3

1. For the purposes set out in Article 2, the activities of the Community shall include, as provided in this Treaty and in accordance with the timetable set out therein:

(a) the prohibition, as between Member States, of customs duties and quantitative restrictions on the import and export of goods, and of all other measures having equivalent effect;

(b) a common commercial policy;

(c) an internal market characterised by the abolition, as between Member States, of obstacles to the free movement of goods, persons, services and capital;

(d) measures concerning the entry and movement of persons as provided for in Title IV;

(e) a common policy in the sphere of agriculture and fisheries;

(f) a common policy in the sphere of transport;

(g) a system ensuring that competition in the internal market is not distorted;

(h) the approximation of the laws of Member States to the extent required for the functioning of the common market;

(i) the promotion of coordination between employment policies of the Member States with a view to enhancing their effectiveness by developing a coordinated strategy for employment;

(j) a policy in the social sphere comprising a European Social Fund;

(k) the strengthening of economic and social cohesion;

(l) a policy in the sphere of the environment;

(m) the strengthening of the competitiveness of Community industry;

(n) the promotion of research and technological development;

(o) encouragement for the establishment and development of trans-European networks;

(p) a contribution to the attainment of a high level of health protection;

(q) a contribution to education and training of quality and to the flowering of the cultures of the Member States;

(r) a policy in the sphere of development cooperation;

(s) the association of the overseas countries and territories in order to increase trade and promote jointly economic and social development;

(t) a contribution to the strengthening of consumer protection;

(u) measures in the spheres of energy, civil protection and tourism.

2. In all the activities referred to in this Article, the Community shall aim to eliminate inequalities, and to promote equality, between men and women.

Article 13

Without prejudice to the other provisions of this Treaty and within the limits of the powers conferred by it upon the Community, the Council, acting unanimously on a proposal from the Commission and after consulting the European Parliament, may take appropriate action to combat discrimination based on sex, racial or ethnic origin, religion or belief, disability, age or sexual orientation.

Article 141

1. Each Member State shall ensure that the principle of equal pay for male and female workers for equal work or work of equal value is applied.

2. For the purpose of this Article, 'pay' means the ordinary basic or minimum wage or salary and any

other consideration, whether in cash or in kind, which the worker receives directly or indirectly, in respect of his employment, from his employer.

Equal pay without discrimination based on sex means:

(a) that pay for the same work at piece rates shall be calculated on the basis of the same unit of measurement;

(b) that pay for work at time rates shall be the same for the same job.

3. The Council, acting in accordance with the procedure referred to in Article 251, and after consulting the Economic and Social Committee, shall adopt measures to ensure the application of the principle of equal opportunities and equal treatment of men and women in matters of employment and occupation, including the principle of equal pay for equal work or work of equal value.

4. With a view to ensuring full equality in practice between men and women in working life, the principle of equal treatment shall not prevent any Member State from maintaining or adopting measures providing for specific advantages in order to make it easier for the under-represented sex to pursue a vocational activity or to prevent or compensate for disadvantages in professional careers.

———————

Council directives

COUNCIL DIRECTIVE 97/80/EC

of 15 December 1997

on the burden of proof in cases of discrimination based on sex

THE COUNCIL OF THE EUROPEAN UNION,

Having regard to the Agreement on social policy annexed to the Protocol (No 14) on social policy annexed to the Treaty establishing the European Community, and in particular Article 2(2) thereof,

Having regard to the proposal from the Commission[1],

Having regard to the opinion of the Economic and Social Committee[2],

Acting, in accordance with the procedure laid down in Article 189c of the Treaty, in cooperation with the European Parliament[3],

(1) Whereas, on the basis of the Protocol on social policy annexed to the Treaty, the Member States, with the exception of the United Kingdom of Great Britain and Northern Ireland (hereinafter called 'the Member States'), wishing to implement the 1989 Social Charter, have concluded an Agreement on social policy;

(2) Whereas the Community Charter of the Fundamental Social Rights of Workers recognises the importance of combating every form of discrimination, including discrimination on grounds of sex, colour, race, opinions and beliefs;

(3) Whereas paragraph 16 of the Community Charter of the Fundamental Social Rights of Workers on equal treatment for men and women, provides, *inter alia,* that 'action should be intensified to ensure the implementation of the principle of equality for men and women as regards, in particular, access to employment, remuneration, working conditions, social protection, education, vocational training and career development';

(4) Whereas, in accordance with Article 3(2) of the Agreement on social policy, the Commission has consulted management and labour at Community level on the possible direction of Community action on the burden of proof in cases of discrimination based on sex;

(5) Whereas the Commission, considering Community action advisable after such consultation, once again consulted management and labour on the content of the proposal contemplated in accordance with Article 3(3) of the same Agreement; whereas the latter have sent their opinions to the Commission;

(6) Whereas, after the second round of consultation, neither management nor labour have informed the Commission of their wish to initiate the process — possibly leading to an agreement — provided for in Article 4 of the same Agreement;

(7) Whereas, in accordance with Article 1 of the Agreement, the Community and the Member States have set themselves the objective, *inter alia,* of improving living and working conditions; whereas effective implementation of the principle of equal treatment for men and women would contribute to the achievement of that aim;

(8) Whereas the principle of equal treatment was stated in Article 119 of the Treaty, in Council Directive 75/117/EEC of 10 February 1975 on the approximation of the laws of the Member States relating to the application of the principle of equal pay for men and women[4] and in Council Directive 76/207/EEC of 9 February 1976 on the implementation of the principle of equal treatment for men and women as regards access to employment, vocational training and promotion and working conditions[5];

(9) Whereas Council Directive 92/85/EEC of 19 October 1992 on the introduction of measures to encourage improvements in the safety and health at work of pregnant workers and workers who have recently given birth or are breastfeeding[6] also contributes to the effective implementation of the principle of equal treatment for men and women; whereas that Directive should not work to the detriment of the aforementioned Directives on equal treatment; whereas, therefore, female workers covered by that Directive should likewise benefit from the adaptation of the rules on the burden of proof;

(10) Whereas Council Directive 96/34/EC of 3 June 1996 on the framework agreement on parental leave concluded by UNICE, CEEP and the

---

[1] OJ C 332, 7.11.1996, p. 11 and
OJ C 185, 18.6.1997, p. 21.

[2] OJ C 133, 28.4.1997, p. 34.

[3] Opinion of the European Parliament of 10 April 1997 (OJ C 132, 28.4.1997, p. 215), Common Position of the Council of 24 July 1997 (OJ C 307, 8.10.1997, p. 6) and Decision of the European Parliament of 6 November 1997 (OJ C 358, 24.11.1997).

---

[4] OJ L 45, 19.2.1975, p. 19.

[5] OJ L 39, 14.2.1976, p. 40.

[6] OJ L 348, 28.11.1992, p. 1.

ETUC(¹), is also based on the principle of equal treatment for men and women;

(11) Whereas the references to 'judicial process' and 'court' cover mechanisms by means of which disputes may be submitted for examination and decision to independent bodies which may hand down decisions that are binding on the parties to those disputes;

(12) Whereas the expression 'out-of-court procedures' means in particular procedures such as conciliation and mediation;

(13) Whereas the appreciation of the facts from which it may be presumed that there has been direct or indirect discrimination is a matter for national judicial or other competent bodies, in accordance with national law or practice;

(14) Whereas it is for the Member States to introduce, at any appropriate stage of the proceedings, rules of evidence which are more favourable to plaintiffs;

(15) Whereas it is necessary to take account of the specific features of certain Member States' legal systems, *inter alia* where an inference of discrimination is drawn if the respondent fails to produce evidence that satisfies the court or other competent authority that there has been no breach of the principle of equal treatment;

(16) Whereas Member States need not apply the rules on the burden of proof to proceedings in which it is for the court or other competent body to investigate the facts of the case; whereas the procedures thus referred to are those in which the plaintiff is not required to prove the facts, which it is for the court or competent body to investigate;

(17) Whereas plaintiffs could be deprived of any effective means of enforcing the principle of equal treatment before the national courts if the effect of introducing evidence of an apparent discrimination were not to impose upon the respondent the burden of proving that his practice is not in fact discriminatory;

(18) Whereas the Court of Justice of the European Communities has therefore held that the rules on the burden of proof must be adapted when there is a prima facie case of discrimination and that, for the principle of equal treatment to be applied effectively, the burden of proof must shift back to the respondent when evidence of such discrimination is brought;

(19) Whereas it is all the more difficult to prove discrimination when it is indirect; whereas it is therefore important to define indirect discrimination;

(20) Whereas the aim of adequately adapting the rules on the burden of proof has not been achieved satisfactorily in all Member States and, in accordance with the principle of subsidiarity stated in Article 3b of the Treaty and with that of proportionality, that aim must be attained at Community level; whereas this Directive confines itself to the minimum action required and does not go beyond what is necessary for that purpose,

HAS ADOPTED THIS DIRECTIVE:

Article 1

Aim

The aim of this Directive shall be to ensure that the measures taken by the Member States to implement the principle of equal treatment are made more effective, in order to enable all persons who consider themselves wronged because the principle of equal treatment has not been applied to them to have their rights asserted by judicial process after possible recourse to other competent bodies.

Article 2

Definitions

1.   For the purposes of this Directive, the principle of equal treatment shall mean that there shall be no discrimination whatsoever based on sex, either directly or indirectly.

2.   For purposes of the principle of equal treatment referred to in paragraph 1, indirect discrimination shall exist where an apparently neutral provision, criterion or practice disadvantages a substantially higher proportion of the members of one sex unless that provision, criterion or practice is appropriate and necessary and can be justified by objective factors unrelated to sex.

Article 3

Scope

1.   This Directive shall apply to:

(a) the situations covered by Article 119 of the Treaty and by Directives 75/117/EEC, 76/207/EEC and, insofar as discrimination based on sex is concerned, 92/85/EEC and 96/34/EC;

(b) any civil or administrative procedure concerning the public or private sector which provides for

---

(¹) OJ L 145, 19.6.1996, p. 4.

means of redress under national law pursuant to the measures referred to in (a) with the exception of out-of-court procedures of a voluntary nature or provided for in national law.

2. This Directive shall not apply to criminal procedures, unless otherwise provided by the Member States.

Article 4

Burden of proof

1. Member States shall take such measures as are necessary, in accordance with their national judicial systems, to ensure that, when persons who consider themselves wronged because the principle of equal treatment has not been applied to them establish, before a court or other competent authority, facts from which it may be presumed that there has been direct or indirect discrimination, it shall be for the respondent to prove that there has been no breach of the principle of equal treatment.

2. This Directive shall not prevent Member States from introducing rules of evidence which are more favourable to plaintiffs.

3. Member States need not apply paragraph 1 to proceedings in which it is for the court or competent body to investigate the facts of the case.

Article 5

Information

Member States shall ensure that measures taken pursuant to this Directive, together with the provisions already in force, are brought to the attention of all the persons concerned by all appropriate means.

Article 6

Non-regression

Implementation of this Directive shall under no circumstances be sufficient grounds for a reduction in the general level of protection of workers in the areas to which it applies, without prejudice to the Member States' right to respond to changes in the situation by introducing laws, regulations and administrative provisions which differ from those in force on the notification of this Directive, provided that the minimum requirements of this Directive are complied with.

Article 7

Implementation

The Member States shall bring into force the laws, regulations and administrative provisions necessary for them to comply with this Directive by 1 January 2001. They shall immediately inform the Commission thereof.

When the Member States adopt those measures they shall contain a reference to this Directive or shall be accompanied by such a reference on the occasion of their official publication. The methods of making such references shall be laid down by the Member States.

The Member States shall communicate to the Commission, within two years of the entry into force of this Directive, all the information necessary for the Commission to draw up a report to the European Parliament and the Council on the application of this Directive.

Article 8

This Directive is addressed to the Member States.

Done at Brussels, 15 December 1997.

For the Council
The President
J.-C. JUNCKER

COUNCIL DIRECTIVE 97/75/EC

of 15 December 1997

amending and extending, to the United Kingdom of Great Britain and Northern Ireland, Directive 96/34/EC on the framework agreement on parental leave concluded by UNICE, CEEP and the ETUC

THE COUNCIL OF THE EUROPEAN UNION,

Having regard to the Treaty establishing the European Community, and in particular Article 100 thereof,

Having regard to the proposal from the Commission [1],

Having regard to the opinion of the European Parliament [2],

Having regard to the opinion of the Economic and Social Committee [3],

Whereas the Council, acting in accordance with the Agreement on social policy annexed to Protocol 14 to the Treaty, and in particular Article 4(2) thereof, adopted Directive 96/34/EC [4]; whereas, as a result, the said Directive does not apply to the United Kingdom of Great Britain and Northern Ireland;

Whereas the Amsterdam European Council, held on 16 and 17 June 1997, noted with approval the agreement of the Intergovernmental Conference to incorporate the Agreement on social policy in the Treaty and also noted that a means had to be found to give legal effect to the wish of the United Kingdom of Great Britain and Northern Ireland to accept the Directives already adopted on the basis of that Agreement before the signature of the Amsterdam Treaty; whereas this Directive seeks to achieve this aim by extending Directive 96/34/EC to the United Kingdom;

Whereas the fact that Directive 96/34/EC is not applicable in the United Kingdom directly affects the functioning of the internal market; whereas implementation of the framework agreement annexed to the said Directive and, in particular, the principle of reconciliation of parental and professional responsibilities for working parents, in all the Member States will improve the functioning of the internal market;

Whereas implementation of the framework agreement aims, in particular, at achieving the objective of equal treatment between men and women with regard to labour opportunities and treatment at work, and the reconciliation of working and family life;

Whereas the adoption of this Directive will make Directive 96/34/EC applicable in the United Kingdom; whereas, from the date on which this Directive enters into force, the term 'Member States' in Directive 96/34/EC should be construed as including the United Kingdom,

HAS ADOPTED THIS DIRECTIVE:

Article 1

Without prejudice to Article 2, Directive 96/34/EC shall apply to the United Kingdom of Great Britain and Northern Ireland.

Article 2

The following paragraph shall be inserted in Article 2 of Directive 96/34/EC:

'1a. As regards the United Kingdom of Great Britain and Northern Ireland, the date of 3 June 1998 in paragraph 1 shall be replaced by 15 December 1999.'

Article 3

This Directive is addressed to the Member States.

Done at Brussels, 15 December 1997.

For the Council
The President
J.-C. JUNCKER

---

[1] OJ C 335, 6.11.1997.
[2] OJ C 371, 8.12.1997.
[3] OJ C 355, 21.11.1997.
[4] OJ L 145, 19.6.1996, p. 4.

COUNCIL DIRECTIVE 96/97/EC

of 20 December 1996

amending Directive 86/378/EEC on the implementation of the principle of equal treatment for men and women in occupational social security schemes

THE COUNCIL OF THE EUROPEAN UNION,

Having regard to the Treaty establishing the European Community, and in particular Article 100 thereof,

Having regard to the proposal from the Commission[1],

Having regard to the opinion of the European Parliament[2],

Having regard to the opinion of the Economic and Social Committee[3],

Whereas Article 119 of the Treaty provides that each Member State shall ensure the application of the principle that men and women should receive equal pay for equal work; whereas 'pay' should be taken to mean the ordinary basic or minimum wage or salary and any other consideration, whether in cash or in kind, which the worker receives, directly or indirectly, from his employer in respect of his employment;

Whereas, in its judgement of 17 May 1990, in Case 262/88: Barber v. Guardian Royal Exchange Assurance Group[4], the Court of Justice of the European Communities acknowledges that all forms of occupational pension constitute an element of pay within the meaning of Article 119 of the Treaty;

Whereas, in the abovementioned judgment, as clarified by the judgment of 14 December 1993 (Case C-110/91: Moroni v. Collo GmbH)[5], the Court interprets Article 119 of the Treaty in such a way that discrimination between men and women in occupational social security schemes is prohibited in general and not only in respect of establishing the age of entitlement to a pension or when an occupational pension is offered by way of compensation for compulsory retirement on economic grounds;

Whereas, in accordance with Protocol 2 concerning Article 119 of the Treaty annexed to the Treaty establishing the European Community, benefits under occupational social security schemes shall not be considered as remuneration if and in so far as they are attributable to periods of employment prior to 17 May 1990, except in the case of workers or those claiming under them who have, before that date, initiated legal proceedings or raised an equivalent claim under the applicable national law;

Whereas, in its judgments of 28 September 1994[6] (Case C-57/93: Vroege v. NCIV Instituut voor Volkshuisvesting BV and Case C-128/93: Fisscher v. Voorhuis Hengelo BV), the Court ruled that the abovementioned Protocol did not affect the right to join an occupational pension scheme, which continues to be governed by the judgment of 13 May 1986 in Case 170/84: Bilka-Kaufhaus GmbH v. Hartz[7], and that the limitation of the effects in time of the judgment of 17 May 1990 in Case C-262/88: Barber v. Guardian Royal Exchange Assurance Group does not apply to the right to join an occupational pension scheme; whereas the Court also ruled that the national rules relating to time limits for bringing actions under national law may be relied on against workers who assert their right to join an occupational pension scheme, provided that they are not less favourable for that type of action than for similar actions of a domestic nature and that they do not render the exercise of rights conferred by Community law impossible in practice; whereas the Court has also pointed out that the fact that a worker can claim retroactively to join an occupational pension scheme does not allow the worker to avoid paying the contributions relating to the period of membership concerned;

Whereas the exclusion of workers on the grounds of the nature of their work contracts from access to a company or sectorial social security scheme may constitute indirect discrimination against women;

Whereas, in its judgment of 9 November 1993 (Case C-132/92: Birds Eye Walls Ltd v. Friedel M. Roberts)[8], the Court has also specified that it is not contrary to Article 119 of the Treaty, when calculating the amount of a bridging pension which is paid by an employer to male and female employees who have taken early retirement on grounds of ill health and which is intended to compensate, in particular, for loss of income resulting from the fact that they have not yet reached the age required for payment of the State pension which they will subsequently receive and to reduce the amount of the bridging pension accordingly, even though, in the case of men and women aged between 60 and 65, the result is that a female ex-employee receives a smaller bridging pension than that paid to her male counterpart, the difference being equal

[1] OJ C 218, 23.8.1995, p. 5.
[2] Opinion delivered on 12 November 1996 (OJ C 362, 2.12.1996).
[3] OJ C 18, 22.1.1996, p. 132.
[4] [1990] ECR I-1889.
[5] [1993] ECR I-6591.

[6] [1994] ECR I-4541 and (1994) ECR I-4583, respectively.
[7] [1986] ECR I-1607.
[8] [1993] ECR I-5579.

to the amount of the State pension to which she is entitled as from the age of 60 in respect of the periods of service completed with that employer;

Whereas, in its judgment of 6 October 1993 (Case C-109/91: Ten Oever v. Stichting Bedrijfpensioen-fonds voor het Glazenwassers- en Schoonmaak-bedrijf)(¹) and in its judgments of 14 December 1993 (Case C-110/91: Moroni v. Collo GmbH), 22 December 1993 (Case C-152/91: Neath v. Hugh Steeper Ltd)(²) and 28 September 1994 (Case C-200/91: Coloroll Pension Trustees Limited v. Russell and Others)(³), the Court confirms that, by virtue of the judgment of 17 May 1990 (Case C-262/88: Barber v. Guardian Royal Exchange Assurance Group), the direct effect of Article 119 of the Treaty may be relied on, for the purpose of claiming equal treatment in the matter of occupational pensions, only in relation to benefits payable in respect of periods of service subsequent to 17 May 1990, except in the case of workers or those claiming under them who have, before that date, initiated legal proceedings or raised an equivalent claim under the applicable national law;

Whereas, in its abovementioned judgments (Case C-109/91: Ten Oever v. Stichting Bedrijfpensioen-fonds voor het Glazenwassers- en Schoonmaakbedrijf and Case C-200/91: Coloroll Pension Trustees Limited v. Russell and Others), the Court confirms that the limitation of the effects in time of the Barber judgment applies to survivors' pensions and, consequently, equal treatment in this matter may be claimed only in relation to periods of service subsequent to 17 May 1990, except in the case of those who have, before that date, initiated legal proceedings or raised an equivalent claim under the applicable national law;

Whereas, moreover, in its judgments in Case C-152/91 and Case C-200/91, the Court specifies that the contributions of male and female workers to a defined-benefit pension scheme must be the same, since they are covered by Article 119 of the Treaty, whereas inequality of employers' contributions paid under funded defined-benefit schemes, which is due to the use of actuarial factors differing according to sex, is not to be assessed in the light of that same provision;

Whereas, in its judgments of 28 September 1994(⁴) (Case C-408/92: Smith v. Advel Systems and Case C-28/93: Van den Akker v. Stichting Shell Pensioen-fonds), the Court points out that Article 119 of the Treaty precludes an employer who adopts measures necessary to comply with the Barber judgment of 17 May 1990 (C-262/88) from raising the retirement age for women to that which exists for men in relation to periods of service completed between 17 May 1990 and the date on which those measures come into force; on the other hand, as regards periods of service completed after the latter date, Article 119 does not prevent an employer from taking that step; as regards periods of service prior to 17 May 1990, Community law imposed no obligation which would justify retroactive reduction of the advantages which women enjoyed;

Whereas, in its abovementioned judgment in Case C-200/91: Coloroll Pension Trustees Limited v. Russell and Others), the Court ruled that additional benefits stemming from contributions paid by employees on a purely voluntary basis are not covered by Article 119 of the Treaty;

Whereas, among the measures included in its third medium-term action programme on equal opportunities for women and men (1991 to 1995)(⁵), the Commission emphasises once more the adoption of suitable measures to take account of the consequences of the judgment of 17 May 1990 in Case 262/88 (Barber v. Guardian Royal Exchange Assurance Group);

Whereas that judgment automatically invalidates certain provisions of Council Directive 86/378/EEC of 24 July 1986 on the implementation of the principle of equal treatment for men and women in occupational social security schemes(⁶) in respect of paid workers;

Whereas Article 119 of the Treaty is directly applicable and can be invoked before the national courts against any employer, whether a private person or a legal person, and whereas it is for these courts to safeguard the rights which that provision confers on individuals;

Whereas, on grounds of legal certainty, it is necessary to amend Directive 86/378/EEC in order to adapt the provisions which are affected by the Barber case-law,

HAS ADOPTED THIS DIRECTIVE:

Article 1

Directive 86/378/EEC shall be amended as follows:

1. Article 2 shall be replaced by the following:

    '*Article 2*

    1. "Occupational social security schemes" means schemes not governed by Directive 79/7/EEC whose purpose is to provide workers, whether employees or self-employed, in an undertaking or group of undertakings, area of economic activity, occupational sector or group of sectors with benefits intended to supplement the benefits provided by statutory social security schemes or to replace them, whether membership of such schemes is compulsory or optional.

(¹) [1993] ECR I-4879.
(²) [1993] ECR I-6953.
(³) [1994] ECR I-4389.
(⁴) [1994] ECR I-4435 and [1994] ECR I-4527, respectively.

(⁵) OJ C 142, 31.5.1991, p. 1.
(⁶) OJ L 225, 12.8.1986, p. 40.

2. This Directive does not apply to:

(a) individual contracts for self-employed workers;

(b) schemes for self-employed workers having only one member;

(c) insurance contracts to which the employer is not a party, in the case of salaried workers;

(d) optional provisions of occupational schemes offered to participants individually to guarantee them:

— either additional benefits, or

— a choice of date on which the normal benefits for self-employed workers will start, or a choice between several benefits;

(e) occupational schemes in so far as benefits are financed by contributions paid by workers on a voluntary basis.

3. This Directive does not preclude an employer granting to persons who have already reached the retirement age for the purposes of granting a pension by virtue of an occupational scheme, but who have not yet reached the retirement age for the purposes of granting a statutory retirement pension, a pension supplement, the aim of which is to make equal or more nearly equal the overall amount of benefit paid to these persons in relation to the amount paid to persons of the other sex in the same situation who have already reached the statutory retirement age, until the persons benefiting from the supplement reach the statutory retirement age.'

2. Article 3 shall be replaced by the following:

'Article 3

This Directive shall apply to members of the working population, including self-employed persons, persons whose activity is interrupted by illness, maternity, accident or involuntary unemployment and persons seeking employment, to retired and disabled workers and to those claiming under them, in accordance with national law and/or practice.'

3. Article 6 shall be replaced by the following:

'Article 6

1. Provisions contrary to the principle of equal treatment shall include those based on sex, either directly or indirectly, in particular by reference to marital or family status, for:

(a) determining the persons who may participate in an occupational scheme;

(b) fixing the compulsory or optional nature of participation in an occupational scheme;

(c) laying down different rules as regards the age of entry into the scheme or the minimum period of employment or membership of the scheme required to obtain the benefits thereof;

(d) laying down different rules, except as provided for in points (h) and (i), for the reimbursement of contributions when a worker leaves a scheme without having fulfilled the conditions guaranteeing a deferred right to long-term benefits;

(e) setting different conditions for the granting of benefits or restricting such benefits to workers of one or other of the sexes;

(f) fixing different retirement ages;

(g) suspending the retention or acquisition of rights during periods of maternity leave or leave for family reasons which are granted by law or agreement and are paid by the employer;

(h) setting different levels of benefit, except in so far as may be necessary to take account of actuarial calculation factors which differ according to sex in the case of defined-contribution schemes.

In the case of funded defined-benefit schemes, certain elements (examples of which are annexed) may be unequal where the inequality of the amounts results from the effects of the use of actuarial factors differing according to sex at the time when the scheme's funding is implemented;

(i) setting different levels for workers' contributions;

setting different levels for employers' contributions, except:

— in the case of defined-contribution schemes if the aim is to equalise the amount of the final benefits or to make them more nearly equal for both sexes,

— in the case of funded defined-benefit schemes where the employer's contributions are intended to ensure the adequacy of the funds necessary to cover the cost of the benefits defined,

(j) laying down different standards or standards applicable only to workers of a specified sex, except as provided for in points (h) and (i), as regards the guarantee or retention of entitlement to deferred benefits when a worker leaves a scheme.

2.   Where the granting of benefits within the scope of this Directive is left to the discretion of the scheme's management bodies, the latter must comply with the principle of equal treatment.'

4.   Article 8 shall be replaced by the following:

'*Article 8*

1.   Member States shall take the necessary steps to ensure that the provisions of occupational schemes for self-employed workers contrary to the principle of equal treatment are revised with effect from 1 January 1993 at the latest.

2.   This Directive shall not preclude rights and obligations relating to a period of membership of an occupational scheme for self-employed workers prior to revision of that scheme from remaining subject to the provisions of the scheme in force during that period.'

5.   Article 9 shall be replaced by the following:

'*Article 9*

As regards schemes for self-employed workers, Member States may defer compulsory application of the principle of equal treatment with regard to:

(a) determination of pensionable age for the granting of old-age or retirement pensions, and the possible implications for other benefits:

— either until the date on which such equality is achieved in statutory schemes,

— or, at the latest, until such equality is prescribed by a directive;

(b) survivors' pensions until Community law establishes the principle of equal treatment in statutory social security schemes in that regard;

(c) the application of the first subparagraph of point (i) of Article 6 (1) to take account of the different actuarial calculation factors, at the latest until 1 January 1999.'

6.   The following Article shall be inserted:

'*Article 9a*

Where men and women may claim a flexible pensionable age under the same conditions, this

shall not be deemed to be incompatible with this Directive.'

7.   The following Annex shall be added:

'ANNEX

Examples of elements which may be unequal, in respect of funded defined-benefit schemes, as referred to in Article 6 (h):

— conversion into a capital sum of part of a periodic pension,

— transfer of pension rights,

— a reversionary pension payable to a dependant in return for the surrender of part of a pension,

— a reduced pension where the worker opts to take early retirement.'

Article 2

1.   Any measure implementing this Directive, as regards paid workers, must cover all benefits derived from periods of employment subsequent to 17 May 1990 and shall apply retroactively to that date, without prejudice to workers or those claiming under them who have, before that date, initiated legal proceedings or raised an equivalent claim under national law. In that event, the implementation measures must apply retroactively to 8 April 1976 and must cover all the benefits derived from periods of employment after that date. For Member States which acceded to the Community after 8 April 1976, that date shall be replaced by the date on which Article 119 of the Treaty became applicable on their territory.

2.   The second sentence of paragraph 1 shall not prevent national rules relating to time limits for bringing actions under national law from being relied on against workers or those claiming under them who initiated legal proceedings or raise an equivalent claim under national law before 17 May 1990, provided that they are not less favourable for that type of action than for similar actions of a domestic nature and that they do not render the exercise of Community law impossible in practice.

3.   For Member States whose accession took place after 17 May 1990 and who were on 1 January 1994 Contracting Parties to the Agreement on the European Economic Area, the date of 17 May 1990 in paragraph 1 and 2 of this Directive is replaced by 1 January 1994.

Article 3

1.   Member States shall bring into force the laws, regulations and administrative provisions necessary to

comply with this Directive by 1 July 1997. They shall forthwith inform the Commission thereof.

When Member States adopt these provisions, they shall contain a reference to this Directive or be accompanied by such reference on the occasion of their official publication. The methods of making such a reference shall be laid down by the Member States.

2.   Member States shall communicate to the Commission, at the latest two years after the entry into force of this Directive, all information necessary to enable the Commission to draw up a report on the application of this Directive.

Article 4

This Directive shall enter into force on the 20th day following that of its publication in the *Official Journal of the European Communities.*

Article 5

This Directive is addressed to the Member States.

Done at Brussels, 20 December 1996.

For the Council

The President

S. BARRETT

COUNCIL DIRECTIVE 96/34/EC

of 3 June 1996

on the framework agreement on parental leave concluded by UNICE, CEEP and the ETUC

THE COUNCIL OF THE EUROPEAN UNION,

Having regard to the Agreement on social policy, annexed to the Protocol (No 14) on social policy, annexed to the Treaty establishing the European Community, and in particular Article 4 (2) thereof,

Having regard to the proposal from the Commission,

(1) Whereas on the basis of the Protocol on social policy, the Member States, with the exception of the United Kingdom of Great Britain and Northern Ireland, (hereinafter referred to as 'the Member States'), wishing to pursue the course mapped out by the 1989 Social Charter have concluded an Agreement on social policy amongst themselves;

(2) Whereas management and labour may, in accordance with Article 4 (2) of the Agreement on social policy, request jointly that agreements at Community level be implemented by a Council decision on a proposal from the Commission;

(3) Whereas paragraph 16 of the Community Charter of the Fundamental Social Rights of Workers on equal treatment for men and women provides, *inter alia,* that 'measures should also be developed enabling men and women to reconcile their occupational and family obligations';

(4) Whereas the Council, despite the existence of a broad consensus, has not been able to act on the proposal for a Directive on parental leave for family reasons([1]), as amended([2]) on 15 November 1984;

(5) Whereas the Commission, in accordance with Article 3 (2) of the Agreement on social policy, consulted management and labour on the possible direction of Community action with regard to reconciling working and family life;

(6) Whereas the Commission, considering after such consultation that Community action was desirable, once again consulted management and labour on the substance of the envisaged proposal in accordance with Article 3 (3) of the said Agreement;

(7) Whereas the general cross-industry organisations (UNICE, CEEP and the ETUC) informed the Commission in their joint letter of 5 July 1995 of their desire to initiate the procedure provided for by Article 4 of the said Agreement;

(8) Whereas the said cross-industry organisations concluded, on 14 December 1995, a framework agreement on parental leave; whereas they have forwarded to the Commission their joint request to implement this framework agreement by a Council Decision on a proposal from the Commission in accordance with Article 4 (2) of the said Agreement;

(9) Whereas the Council, in its Resolution of 6 December 1994 on certain aspects for a European Union social policy; a contribution to economic and social convergence in the Union([3]), asked the two sides of industry to make use of the possibilities for concluding agreements, since they are as a rule closer to social reality and to social problems; whereas in Madrid, the members of the European Council from those States which have signed the Agreement on social policy welcomed the conclusion of this framework agreement;

(10) Whereas the signatory parties wanted to conclude a framework agreement setting out minimum requirements on parental leave and time off from work on grounds of *force majeure* and referring back to the Member States and/or management and labour for the definition of the conditions under which parental leave would be implemented, in order to take account of the situation, including the situation with regard to family policy, existing in each Member State, particularly as regards the conditions for granting parental leave and exercise of the right to parental leave;

(11) Whereas the proper instrument for implementing this framework agreement is a Directive within the meaning of Article 189 of the Treaty; whereas it is therefore binding on the Member States as to the result to be achieved, but leaves them the choice of form and methods;

(12) Whereas, in keeping with the principle of subsidiarity and the principle of proportionality as set out in Article 3b of the Treaty, the objectives of this Directive cannot be sufficiently achieved by the Member States and can therefore be better achieved by the Community; whereas this Directive is confined to the minimum required to

---

([1]) OJ C 333, 9.12.1983, p. 6.
([2]) OJ C 316, 27.11.1984, p. 7.
([3]) OJ C 368, 23.12.1994, p. 6.

achieve these objectives and does not go beyond what is necessary to achieve that purpose;

(13) Whereas the Commission has drafted its proposal for a Directive, taking into account the representative status of the signatory parties, their mandate and the legality of the clauses of the framework agreement and compliance with the relevant provisions concerning small and medium-sized undertakings;

(14) Whereas the Commission, in accordance with its Communication of 14 December 1993 concerning the implementation of the Protocol on social policy, informed the European Parliament by sending it the text of the framework agreement, accompanied by its proposal for a Directive and the explanatory memorandum;

(15) Whereas the Commission also informed the Economic and Social Committee by sending it the text of the framework agreement, accompanied by its proposal for a Directive and the explanatory memorandum;

(16) Whereas clause 4 point 2 of the framework agreement states that the implementation of the provisions of this agreement does not constitute valid grounds for reducing the general level of protection afforded to workers in the field of this agreement. This does not prejudice the right of Member States and/or management and labour to develop different legislative, regulatory or contractual provisions, in the light of changing circumstances (including the introduction of non-transferability), as long as the minimum requirements provided for in the present agreement are complied with;

(17) Whereas the Community Charter of the Fundamental Social Rights of Workers recognises the importance of the fight against all forms of discrimination, especially based on sex, colour, race, opinions and creeds;

(18) Whereas Article F (2) of the Treaty on European Union provides that 'the Union shall respect fundamental rights, as guaranteed by the European Convention for the Protection of Human Rights and Fundamental Freedoms signed in Rome on 4 November 1950 and as they result from the constitutional traditions common to the Member States, as general principles of Community law';

(19) Whereas the Member States can entrust management and labour, at their joint request, with the implementation of this Directive, as long as they take all the necessary steps to ensure that they can at all times guarantee the results imposed by this Directive;

(20) Whereas the implementation of the framework agreement contributes to achieving the objectives under Article 1 of the Agreement on social policy,

HAS ADOPTED THIS DIRECTIVE:

Article 1

Implementation of the framework agreement

The purpose of this Directive is to put into effect the annexed framework agreement on parental leave concluded on 14 December 1995 between the general cross-industry organisations (UNICE, CEEP and the ETUC).

Article 2

Final provisions

1. The Member States shall bring into force the laws, regulations and administrative provisions necessary to comply with this Directive by 3 June 1998 at the latest or shall ensure by that date at the latest that management and labour have introduced the necessary measures by agreement, the Member States being required to take any necessary measure enabling them at any time to be in a position to guarantee the results imposed by this Directive. They shall forthwith inform the Commission thereof.

2. The Member States may have a maximum additional period of one year, if this is necessary to take account of special difficulties or implementation by a collective agreement.

They must forthwith inform the Commission of such circumstances.

3. When Member States adopt the measures referred to in paragraph 1, they shall contain a reference to this Directive or be accompanied by such reference on the occasion of their official publication. The methods of making such reference shall be laid down by Member States.

Article 3

This Directive is addressed to the Member States.

Done at Luxembourg, 3 June 1996.

For the Council
The President
T. TREU

FRAMEWORK AGREEMENT ON PARENTAL LEAVE

PREAMBLE

The enclosed framework agreement represents an undertaking by UNICE, CEEP and the ETUC to set out minimum requirements on parental leave and time off from work on grounds of *force majeure,* as an important means of reconciling work and family life and promoting equal opportunities and treatment between men and women.

ETUC, UNICE and CEEP request the Commission to submit this framework agreement to the Council for a Council Decision making these minimum requirements binding in the Member States of the European Community, with the exception of the United Kingdom of Great Britain and Northern Ireland.

I. GENERAL CONSIDERATIONS

1. Having regard to the Agreement on social policy annexed to the Protocol on social policy, annexed to the Treaty establishing the European Community, and in particular Articles 3 (4) and 4 (2) thereof;

2. Whereas Article 4 (2) of the Agreement on social policy provides that agreements concluded at Community level shall be implemented, at the joint request of the signatory parties, by a Council decision on a proposal from the Commission;

3. Whereas the Commission has announced its intention to propose a Community measure on the reconciliation of work and family life;

4. Whereas the Community Charter of Fundamental Social Rights stipulates at point 16 dealing with equal treatment that measures should be developed to enable men and women to reconcile their occupational and family obligations;

5. Whereas the Council Resolution of 6 December 1994 recognises that an effective policy of equal opportunities presupposes an integrated overall strategy allowing for better organisation of working hours and greater flexibility, and for an easier return to working life, and notes the important role of the two sides of industry in this area and in offering both men and women an opportunity to reconcile their work responsibilities with family obligations;

6. Whereas measures to reconcile work and family life should encourage the introduction of new flexible ways of organising work and time which are better suited to the changing needs of society and which should take the needs of both undertakings and workers into account;

7. Whereas family policy should be looked at in the context of demographic changes, the effects of the ageing population, closing the generation gap and promoting women's participation in the labour force;

8. Whereas men should be encouraged to assume an equal share of family responsibilities, for example they should be encouraged to take parental leave by means such as awareness programmes;

9. Whereas the present agreement is a framework agreement setting out minimum requirements and provisions for parental leave, distinct from maternity leave, and for time off from work on grounds of *force majeure,* and refers back to Member States and social partners for the establishment of the conditions of access and detailed rules of application in order to take account of the situation in each Member State;

10. Whereas Member States should provide for the maintenance of entitlements to benefits in kind under sickness insurance during the minimum period of parental leave;

11. Whereas Member States should also, where appropriate under national conditions and taking into account the budgetary situation, consider the maintenance of entitlements to relevant social security benefits as they stand during the minimum period of parental leave;

12. Whereas this agreement takes into consideration the need to improve social policy requirements, to enhance the competitiveness of the Community economy and to avoid imposing administrative, financial and legal constraints in a way which would impede the creation and development of small and medium-sized undertakings;

13. Whereas management and labour are best placed to find solutions that correspond to the needs of both employers and workers and must therefore have conferred on them a special role in the implementation and application of the present agreement,

THE SIGNATORY PARTIES HAVE AGREED THE FOLLOWING:

II. CONTENT

Clause 1: **Purpose and scope**

1. This agreement lays down minimum requirements designed to facilitate the reconciliation of parental and professional responsibilities for working parents.

2. This agreement applies to all workers, men and women, who have an employment contract or employment relationship as defined by the law, collective agreements or practices in force in each Member State.

Clause 2: **Parental leave**

1. This agreement grants, subject to clause 2.2, men and women workers an individual right to parental leave on the grounds of the birth or adoption of a child to enable them to take care of that child, for at least three months, until a given age up to 8 years to be defined by Member States and/or management and labour.

2. To promote equal opportunities and equal treatment between men and women, the parties to this agreement consider that the right to parental leave provided for under clause 2.1 should, in principle, be granted on a non-transferable basis.

3. The conditions of access and detailed rules for applying parental leave shall be defined by law and/or collective agreement in the Member States, as long as the minimum requirements of this agreement are respected. Member States and/or management and labour may, in particular:

   (a) decide whether parental leave is granted on a full-time or part-time basis, in a piecemeal way or in the form of a time-credit system;

   (b) make entitlement to parental leave subject to a period of work qualification and/or a length of service qualification which shall not exceed one year;

   (c) adjust conditions of access and detailed rules for applying parental leave to the special circumstances of adoption;

   (d) establish notice periods to be given by the worker to the employer when exercising the right to parental leave, specifying the beginning and the end of the period of leave;

   (e) define the circumstances in which an employer, following consultation in accordance with national law, collective agreements and practices, is allowed to postpone the granting of parental leave for justifiable reasons related to the operation of the undertaking (e.g. where work is of a seasonal nature, where a replacement cannot be found within the notice period, where a significant proportion of the workforce applies for parental leave at the same time, where a specific function is of strategic importance). Any problem arising from the application of this provision should be dealt with in accordance with national law, collective agreements and practices;

(f) in addition to (e), authorise special arrangements to meet the operational and organisational requirements of small undertakings.

4. In order to ensure that workers can exercise their right to parental leave, Member States and/or management and labour shall take the necessary measures to protect workers against dismissal on the grounds of an application for, or the taking of, parental leave in accordance with national law, collective agreements or practices.

5. At the end of parental leave, workers shall have the right to return to the same job or, if that is not possible, to an equivalent or similar job consistent with their employment contract or employment relationship.

6. Rights acquired or in the process of being acquired by the worker on the date on which parental leave starts shall be maintained as they stand until the end of parental leave. At the end of parental leave, these rights, including any changes arising from national law, collective agreements or practice, shall apply.

7. Member States and/or management and labour shall define the status of the employment contract or employment relationship for the period of parental leave.

8. All matters relating to social security in relation to this agreement are for consideration and determination by Member States according to national law, taking into account the importance of the continuity of the entitlements to social security cover under the different schemes, in particular health care.

Clause 3: **Time off from work on grounds of** *force majeure*

1. Member States and/or management and labour shall take the necessary measures to entitle workers to time off from work, in accordance with national legislation, collective agreements and/or practice, on grounds of *force majeure* for urgent family reasons in cases of sickness or accident making the immediate presence of the worker indispensable.

2. Member States and/or management and labour may specify the conditions of access and detailed rules for applying clause 3.1 and limit this entitlement to a certain amount of time per year and/or per case.

Clause 4: **Final provisions**

1. Member States may apply or introduce more favourable provisions than those set out in this agreement.

2. Implementation of the provisions of this agreement shall not constitute valid grounds for reducing the general level of protection afforded to workers in the field covered by this agreement. This shall not prejudice the right of Member States and/or management and labour to develop different legislative, regulatory or contractual provisions, in the light of changing circumstances (including the introduction of non-transferability), as long as the minimum requirements provided for in the present agreement are complied with.

3. The present agreement shall not prejudice the right of management and labour to conclude, at the appropriate level including European level, agreements adapting and/or complementing the provisions of this agreement in order to take into account particular circumstances.

4. Member States shall adopt the laws, regulations and administrative provisions necessary to comply with the Council decision within a period of two years from its adoption or shall ensure that management and labour (¹) introduce the necessary measures by way of agreement by the end of this period. Member States may, if necessary to take account of particular difficulties or implementation by collective agreement, have up to a maximum of one additional year to comply with this decision.

5. The prevention and settlement of disputes and grievances arising from the application of this agreement shall be dealt with in accordance with national law, collective agreements and practices.

6. Without prejudice to the respective role of the Commission, national courts and the Court of Justice, any matter relating to the interpretation of this agreement at European level should, in the first instance, be referred by the Commission to the signatory parties who will give an opinion.

7. The signatory parties shall review the application of this agreement five years after the date of the Council decision if requested by one of the parties to this agreement.

(¹) Within the meaning of Article 2 (4) of the Agreement on social policy.

Done at Brussels, 14 December 1995.

Fritz VERZETNITSCH,	Antonio Castellano AUYANET,	François PERIGOT,
President of the ETUC	*President of the CEEP*	*President of the UNICE*
Emilio GABAGLIO,	Roger GOURVÈS,	Zygmunt TYSZKIEWICZ,
Secretary-General	*Secretary-General*	*Secretary-General*
ETUC	CEEP	UNICE
Bld Emile Jacqmain 155	Rue de la Charité 15	Rue Joseph II 40
B-1210 Brussels	B-1040 Brussels	B-1040 Brussels

COUNCIL DIRECTIVE 92/85/EEC

of 19 October 1992

on the introduction of measures to encourage improvements in the safety and health at work of pregnant workers and workers who have recently given birth or are breast-feeding (tenth individual Directive within the meaning of Article 16 (1) of Directive 89/391/EEC)

THE COUNCIL OF THE EUROPEAN COMMUNITIES,

Having regard to the Treaty establishing the European Economic Community, and in particular Article 118a thereof,

Having regard to the proposal from the Commission, drawn up after consultation with the Advisory Committee on Safety, Hygiene and Health Protection at work [1],

In cooperation with the European Parliament [2],

Having regard to the opinion of the Economic and Social Committee [3],

Whereas Article 118a of the Treaty provides that the Council shall adopt, by means of directives, minimum requirements for encouraging improvements, especially in the working environment, to protect the safety and health of workers;

Whereas this Directive does not justify any reduction in levels of protection already achieved in individual Member States, the Member States being committed, under the Treaty, to encouraging improvements in conditions in this area and to harmonising conditions while maintaining the improvements made;

Whereas, under the terms of Article 118a of the Treaty, the said directives are to avoid imposing administrative, financial and legal constraints in a way which would hold back the creation and development of small and medium-sized undertakings;

Whereas, pursuant to Decision 74/325/EEC [4], as last amended by the 1985 Act of Accession, the Advisory Committee on Safety, Hygiene and Health protection at Work is consulted by the Commission on the drafting of proposals in this field;

Whereas the Community Charter of the fundamental social rights of workers, adopted at the Strasbourg European Council on 9 December 1989 by the Heads of State or Government of 11 Member States, lays down, in paragraph 19 in particular, that:

'Every worker must enjoy satisfactory health and safety conditions in his working environment. Appropriate measures must be taken in order to achieve further harmonisation of conditions in this area while maintaining the improvements made';

Whereas the Commission, in its action programme for the implementation of the Community Charter of the fundamental social rights of workers, has included among its aims the adoption by the Council of a Directive on the protection of pregnant women at work;

Whereas Article 15 of Council Directive 89/391/EEC of 12 June 1989 on the introduction of measures to encourage improvements in the safety and health of workers at work [5] provides that particularly sensitive risk groups must be protected against the dangers which specifically affect them;

Whereas pregnant workers, workers who have recently given birth or who are breastfeeding must be considered a specific risk group in many respects, and measures must be taken with regard to their safety and health;

Whereas the protection of the safety and health of pregnant workers, workers who have recently given birth or workers who are breastfeeding should not treat women on the labour market unfavourably nor work to the detriment of directives concerning equal treatment for men and women;

Whereas some types of activities may pose a specific risk, for pregnant workers, workers who have recently given birth or workers who are breastfeeding, of exposure to dangerous agents, processes or working conditions; whereas such risks must therefore be assessed and the result of such assessment communicated to female workers and/or their representatives;

Whereas, further, should the result of this assessment reveal the existence of a risk to the safety or health of the female worker, provision must be made for such workers to be protected;

Whereas pregnant workers and workers who are breastfeeding must not engage in activities which have

[1] OJ C 281, 9.11.1990, p. 3; and
OJ C 25, 1.2.1991, p. 9.
[2] OJ C 19, 28.1.1991, p. 177; and
OJ C 150, 15.6.1992, p. 99.
[3] OJ C 41, 18.2.1991, p. 29.
[4] OJ L 185, 9.7.1974, p. 15.

[5] OJ L 183, 29.6.1989, p. 1.

been assessed as revealing a risk of exposure, jeopardising safety and health, to certain particularly dangerous agents or working conditions;

Whereas provision should be made for pregnant workers, workers who have recently given birth or workers who are breastfeeding not to be required to work at night where such provision is necessary from the point of view of their safety and health;

Whereas the vulnerability of pregnant workers, workers who have recently given birth or who are breastfeeding makes it necessary for them to be granted the right to maternity leave of at least 14 continuous weeks, allocated before and/or after confinement, and renders necessary the compulsory nature of maternity leave of at least two weeks, allocated before and/or after confinement;

Whereas the risk of dismissal for reasons associated with their condition may have harmful effects on the physical and mental state of pregnant workers, workers who have recently given birth or who are breastfeeding; whereas provision should be made for such dismissal to be prohibited;

Whereas measures for the organisation of work concerning the protection of the health of pregnant workers, workers who have recently given birth or workers who are breastfeeding would serve no purpose unless accompanied by the maintenance of rights linked to the employment contract, including maintenance of payment and/or entitlement to an adequate allowance;

Whereas, moreover, provision concerning maternity leave would also serve no purpose unless accompanied by the maintenance of rights linked to the employment contract and or entitlement to an adequate allowance;

Whereas the concept of an adequate allowance in the case of maternity leave must be regarded as a technical point of reference with a view to fixing the minimum level of protection and should in no circumstances be interpreted as suggesting an analogy between pregnancy and illness,

HAS ADOPTED THIS DIRECTIVE

SECTION I

PURPOSE AND DEFINITIONS

Article 1

Purpose

1.   The purpose of this Directive, which is the tenth individual Directive within the meaning of Article 16 (1) of Directive 89/391/EEC, is to implement measures to encourage improvements in the safety and health at work of pregnant workers and workers who have recently given birth or who are breastfeeding.

2.   The provisions of Directive 89/391/EEC, except for Article 2 (2) thereof, shall apply in full to the whole area covered by paragraph 1, without prejudice to any more stringent and/or specific provisions contained in this Directive.

3.   This Directive may not have the effect of reducing the level of protection afforded to pregnant workers, workers who have recently given birth or who are breastfeeding as compared with the situation which exists in each Member State on the date on which this Directive is adopted.

Article 2

Definitions

For the purposes of this Directive:

(a) *pregnant worker* shall mean a pregnant worker who informs her employer of her condition, in accordance with national legislation and/or national practice;

(b) *worker who has recently given birth* shall mean a worker who has recently given birth within the meaning of national legislation and/or national practice and who informs her employer of her condition, in accordance with that legislation and/or practice;

(c) *worker who is breastfeeding* shall mean a worker who is breastfeeding within the meaning of national legislation and/or national practice and who informs her employer of her condition, in accordance with that legislation and/or practice.

SECTION II

GENERAL PROVISIONS

Article 3

Guidelines

1.   In consultation with the Member States and assisted by the Advisory Committee on Safety, Hygiene and Health Protection at Work, the Commission shall draw up guidelines on the assessment of the chemical, physical and biological agents and industrial processes considered hazardous for the safety or health of workers within the meaning of Article 2.

The guidelines referred to in the first subparagraph shall also cover movements and postures, mental and physical fatigue and other types of physical and mental stress connected with the work done by workers within the meaning of Article 2.

2.   The purpose of the guidelines referred to in paragraph 1 is to serve as a basis for the assessment referred to in Article 4 (1).

To this end, Member States shall bring these guidelines to the attention of all employers and all female workers and/or their representatives in the respective Member State.

Article 4

Assessment and information

1.   For all activities liable to involve a specific risk of exposure to the agents, processes or working conditions of which a non-exhaustive list is given in Annex I, the employer shall assess the nature, degree and duration of exposure, in the undertaking and/or establishment concerned, of workers within the meaning of Article 2, either directly or by way of the protective and preventive services referred to in Article 7 of Directive 89/391/EEC, in order to:

— assess any risks to the safety or health and any possible effect on the pregnancies or breastfeeding of workers within the meaning of Article 2,

— decide what measures should be taken.

2.   Without prejudice to Article 10 of Directive 89/391/EEC, workers within the meaning of Article 2 and workers likely to be in one of the situations referred to in Article 2 in the undertaking and/or establishment concerned and/or their representatives shall be informed of the results of the assessment referred to in paragraph 1 and of all measures to be taken concerning health and safety at work.

Article 5

Action further to the results of the assessment

1.   Without prejudice to Article 6 of Directive 89/391/EEC, if the results of the assessment referred to in Article 4 (1) reveal a risk to the safety or health or an effect on the pregnancy or breastfeeding of a worker within the meaning of Article 2, the employer shall take the necessary measures to ensure that, by temporarily adjusting the working conditions and/or the working hours of the worker concerned, the exposure of that worker to such risks is avoided.

2.   If the adjustment of her working conditions and/or working hours is not technically and/or objectively feasible, or cannot reasonably be required on duly substantiated grounds, the employer shall take the

necessary measures to move the worker concerned to another job.

3.   If moving her to another job is not technically and/or objectively feasible or cannot reasonably be required on duly substantiated grounds, the worker concerned shall be granted leave in accordance with national legislation and/or national practice for the whole of the period necessary to protect her safety or health.

4.   The provisions of this Article shall apply *mutatis mutandis* to the case where a worker pursuing an activity which is forbidden pursuant to Article 6 becomes pregnant or starts breastfeeding and informs her employer thereof.

Article 6

Cases in which exposure is prohibited

In addition to the general provisions concerning the protection of workers, in particular those relating to the limit values for occupational exposure:

1.   pregnant workers within the meaning of Article 2 (a) may under no circumstances be obliged to perform duties for which the assessment has revealed a risk of exposure, which would jeopardise safety or health, to the agents and working conditions listed in Annex II, Section A;

2.   workers who are breastfeeding, within the meaning of Article 2 (c), may under no circumstances be obliged to perform duties for which the assessment has revealed a risk of exposure, which would jeopardise safety or health, to the agents and working conditions listed in Annex II, Section B.

Article 7

Night work

1.   Member States shall take the necessary measures to ensure that workers referred to in Article 2 are not obliged to perform night work during their pregnancy and for a period following childbirth which shall be determined by the national authority competent for safety and health, subject to submission, in accordance with the procedures laid down by the Member States, of a medical certificate stating that this is necessary for the safety or health of the worker concerned.

2.   The measures referred to in paragraph 1 must entail the possibility, in accordance with national legislation and/or national practice, of:

(a) transfer to daytime work; or

(b) leave from work or extension of maternity leave where such a transfer is not technically and/or objectively feasible or cannot reasonably by required on duly substantiated grounds.

Article 8

Maternity leave

1. Member States shall take the necessary measures to ensure that workers within the meaning of Article 2 are entitled to a continuous period of maternity leave of a least 14 weeks allocated before and/or after confinement in accordance with national legislation and/or practice.

2. The maternity leave stipulated in paragraph 1 must include compulsory maternity leave of at least two weeks allocated before and/or after confinement in accordance with national legislation and/or practice.

Article 9

Time off for ante-natal examinations

Member States shall take the necessary measures to ensure that pregnant workers within the meaning of Article 2 (a) are entitled to, in accordance with national legislation and/or practice, time off, without loss of pay, in order to attend ante-natal examinations, if such examinations have to take place during working hours.

Article 10

Prohibition of dismissal

In order to guarantee workers, within the meaning of Article 2, the exercise of their health and safety protection rights as recognised under this Article, it shall be provided that:

1. Member States shall take the necessary measures to prohibit the dismissal of workers, within the meaning of Article 2, during the period from the beginning of their pregnancy to the end of the maternity leave referred to in Article 8 (1), save in exceptional cases not connected with their condition which are permitted under national legislation and/or practice and, where applicable, provided that the competent authority has given its consent;

2. if a worker, within the meaning of Article 2, is dismissed during the period referred to in point 1, the employer must cite duly substantiated grounds for her dismissal in writing;

3. Member States shall take the necessary measures to protect workers, within the meaning of Article 2, from consequences of dismissal which is unlawful by virtue of point 1.

Article 11

Employment rights

In order to guarantee workers within the meaning of Article 2 the exercise of their health and safety protection rights as recognised in this Article, it shall be provided that:

1. in the cases referred to in Articles 5, 6 and 7, the employment rights relating to the employment contract, including the maintenance of a payment to, and/or entitlement to an adequate allowance for, workers within the meaning of Article 2, must be ensured in accordance with national legislation and/or national practice;

2. in the case referred to in Article 8, the following must be ensured:

   (a) the rights connected with the employment contract of workers within the meaning of Article 2, other than those referred to in point (b) below;

   (b) maintenance of a payment to, and/or entitlement to an adequate allowance for, workers within the meaning of Article 2;

3. the allowance referred to in point 2 (b) shall be deemed adequate if it guarantees income at least equivalent to that which the worker concerned would receive in the event of a break in her activities on grounds connected with her state of health, subject to any ceiling laid down under national legislation;

4. Member States may make entitlement to pay or the allowance referred to in points 1 and 2 (b) conditional upon the worker concerned fulfilling the conditions of eligibilty for such benefits laid down under national legislation.

   These conditions may under no circumstances provide for periods of previous employment in excess of 12 months immediately prior to the presumed date of confinement.

Article 12

Defence of rights

Member States shall introduce into their national legal systems such measures as are necessary to enable all workers who consider themselves wronged by failure to comply with the obligations arising from this Directive to pursue their claims by judicial process (and/or, in accordance with national laws and/or practices) by recourse to other competent authorities.

Article 13

Amendments to the Annexes

1.   Strictly technical adjustments to Annex I as a result of technical progress, changes in international regulations or specifications and new findings in the area covered by this Directive shall be adopted in accordance with the procedure laid down in Article 17 of Directive 89/391/EEC.

2.   Annex II may be amended only in accordance with the procedure laid down in Article 118a of the Treaty.

Article 14

Final provisions

1.   Member States shall bring into force the laws, regulations and administrative provisions necessary to comply with this Directive not later than two years after the adoption thereof or ensure, at the latest two years after adoption of this Directive, that the two sides of industry introduce the requisite provisions by means of collective agreements, with Member States being required to make all the necessary provisions to enable them at all times to guarantee the results laid down by this Directive. They shall forthwith inform the Commission thereof.

2.   When Member States adopt the measures referred to in paragraph 1, they shall contain a reference to this Directive or shall be accompanied by such reference on the occasion of their official publication. The methods of making such a reference shall be laid down by the Member States.

3.   Member States shall communicate to the Commission the texts of the essential provisions of national law which they have already adopted or adopt in the field governed by this Directive.

4.   Member States shall report to the Commission every five years on the practical implementation of the provisions of this Directive, indicating the points of view of the two sides of industry.

However, Member States shall report for the first time to the Commission on the practical implementation of the provisions of this Directive, indicating the points of view of the two sides of industry, four years after its adoption.

The Commission shall inform the European Parliament, the Council, the Economic and Social Committee and the Advisory Committee on Safety, Hygiene and Health Protection at Work.

5.   The Commission shall periodically submit to the European Parliament, the Council and the Economic and Social Committee a report on the implementation of this Directive, taking into account paragraphs 1, 2 and 3.

6.   The Council will re-examine this Directive, on the basis of an assessment carried out on the basis of the reports referred to in the second subparagraph of paragraph 4 and, should the need arise, of a proposal, to be submitted by the Commission at the latest five years after adoption of the Directive.

Article 15

This Directive is addressed to the Member States.

Done at Luxembourg, 19 October 1992.

For the Council
The President
D. CURRY

ANNEX I

NON-EXHAUSTIVE LIST OF AGENTS, PROCESSES AND WORKING CONDITIONS

referred to in Article 4 (1)

A. Agents

1. *Physical agents* where these are regarded as agents causing foetal lesions and/or likely to disrupt placental attachment, and in particular:

   (a) shocks, vibration or movement;

   (b) handling of loads entailing risks, particularly of a dorsolumbar nature;

   (c) noise;

   (d) ionising radiation (*);

   (e) non-ionising radiation;

   (f) extremes of cold or heat;

   (g) movements and postures, travelling — either inside or outside the establishment — mental and physical fatigue and other physical burdens connected with the activity of the worker within the meaning of Article 2 of the Directive.

2. *Biological agents*

   Biological agents of risk groups 2, 3 and 4 within the meaning of Article 2 (d) numbers 2, 3 and 4 of Directive 90/679/EEC (¹), in so far as it is known that these agents or the therapeutic measures necessitated by such agents endanger the health of pregnant women and the unborn child and in so far as they do not yet appear in Annex II.

3. *Chemical agents*

   The following chemical agents in so far as it is known that they endanger the health of pregnant women and the unborn child and in so far as they do not yet appear in Annex II:

   (a) substances labelled R 40, R 45, R 46, and R 47 under Directive 67/548/EEC (²) in so far as they do not yet appear in Annex II;

   (b) chemical agents in Annex I to Directive 90/394/EEC (³);

   (c) mercury and mercury derivatives;

   (d) antimitotic drugs;

   (e) carbon monoxide;

   (f) chemical agents of known and dangerous percutaneous absorption.

B. Processes

Industrial processes listed in Annex I to Directive 90/394/EEC.

C. Working conditions

Underground mining work.

———

(*) See Directive 80/836/Euratom (OJ L 246, 17.9.1980, p. 1).
(¹) OJ L 374, 31.12.1990, p. 1.
(²) OJ L 196, 16.8.1967, p. 1. Directive as last amended by Directive 90/517/EEC (OJ L 287, 19.10.1990, p. 37).
(³) OJ L 196, 26.7.1990, p. 1.

ANNEX II

NON-EXHAUSTIVE LIST OF AGENTS AND WORKING CONDITIONS

referred to in Article 6

A. Pregnant workers within the meaning of Article 2 (a)

1. *Agents*

   (a) Physical agents

   — Work in hyperbaric atmosphere, e.g. pressurised enclosures and underwater diving.

   (b) Biological agents

   The following biological agents:

   — toxoplasma,

   — rubella virus,

   unless the pregnant workers are proved to be adequately protected against such agents by immunisation.

   (c) Chemical agents

   Lead and lead derivatives in so far as these agents are capable of being absorbed by the human organism.

2. *Working conditions*

   Underground mining work.

B. Workers who are breastfeeding within the meaning of Article 2 (c)

1. *Agents*

   (a) Chemical agents

   Lead and lead derivatives in so far as these agents are capable of being absorbed by the human organism.

2. *Working conditions*

   Underground mining work.

————————

Statement of the Council and the Commission concerning Article 11 (3) of Directive 92/85/EEC, entered in the minutes of the 1608th meeting of the Council (Luxembourg, 19 October 1992)

THE COUNCIL AND THE COMMISSION stated that:

In determining the level of the allowances referred to in Article 11 (2) (b) and (3), reference shall be made, for purely technical reasons, to the allowance which a worker would receive in the event of a break in her activities on grounds connected with her state of health. Such a reference is not intended in any way to imply that pregnancy and childbirth be equated with sickness. The national social security legislation of all Member States provides for an allowance to be paid during an absence from work due to sickness. The link with such allowance in the chosen formulation is simply intended to serve as a concrete, fixed reference amount in all Member States for the determination of the minimum amount of maternity allowance payable. In so far as allowances are paid in individual Member States which exceed those provided for in the Directive, such allowances are, of course, retained. This is clear from Article 1 (3) of the Directive.

———

COUNCIL DIRECTIVE (86/613/EEC)

of 11 December 1986

on the application of the principle of equal treatment between men and women engaged in an activity, including agriculture, in a self-employed capacity, and on the protection of self-employed women during pregnancy and motherhood

THE COUNCIL OF THE EUROPEAN COMMUNITIES,

Having regard to the Treaty establishing the European Economic Community, and in particular Articles 100 and 235 thereof,

Having regard to the proposal from the Commission [1],

Having regard to the opinion of the European Parliament [2],

Having regard to the opinion of the Economic and Social Committee [3],

Whereas, in its resolution of 12 July 1982 on the promotion of equal opportunities for women [4], the Council approved the general objectives of the Commission communication concerning a new Community action programme on the promotion of equal opportunities for women (1982 to 1985) and expressed the will to implement appropriate measures to achieve them;

Whereas action 5 of the programme referred to above concerns the application of the principle of equal treatment to self-employed women and to women in agriculture;

Whereas the implementation of the principle of equal pay for men and women workers, as laid down in Article 119 of the Treaty, forms an integral part of the establishment and functioning of the common market;

Whereas on 10 February 1975 the Council adopted Directive 75/117/EEC on the approximation of the laws of the Member States relating to the application of the principle of equal pay for men and women [5];

Whereas, as regards other aspects of equality of treatment between men and women, on 9 February 1976 the Council adopted Directive 76/207/EEC on the implementation of the principle of equal treament for men and women as regards access to employment, vocational training and promotion, and working conditions [6] and on 19 December 1978 Directive 79/7/EEC on the progressive implementation of the principle of equal treatment for men and women in matters of social security [7];

Whereas, as regards persons engaged in a self-employed capacity, in an activity in which their spouses are also engaged, the implementation of the principle of equal treatment should be pursued through the adoption of detailed provisions designed to cover the specific situation of these persons;

Whereas differences persist between the Member States in this field, whereas, therefore it is necessary to approximate national provisions with regard to the application of the principle of equal treatment;

Whereas in certain respects the Treaty does not confer the powers necessary for the specific actions required;

Whereas the implementation of the principle of equal treatment is without prejudice to measures concerning the protection of women during pregnancy and motherhood,

HAS ADOPTED THIS DIRECTIVE:

SECTION I

Aims and scope

Article 1

The purpose of this Directive is to ensure, in accordance with the following provisions, application in the Member States of the principle of equal treatment as between men and women engaged in an activity in a self-employed capacity, or contributing to the pursuit of such an activity, as regards those aspects not covered by Directives 76/207/EEC and 79/7/EEC.

Article 2

This Directive covers:

(a) self-employed workers, i.e. all persons pursuing a gainful activity for their own account, under the conditions laid down by national law, including farmers and members of the liberal professions;

---

[1] OJ C 113, 27.4.1984, p. 4.
[2] OJ C 172, 2.7.1984, p. 90.
[3] OJ C 343, 24.12.1984, p. 1.
[4] OJ C 186, 21.7.1982, p. 3.
[5] OJ L 45, 19.2.1975, p. 19.
[6] OJ L 39, 14.2.1975, p. 40.

---

[7] OJ L 6, 10.1.1979, p. 24.

(b) their spouses, not being employees or partners, where they habitually, under the conditions laid down by national law, participate in the activities of the self-employed worker and perform the same tasks or ancillary tasks.

Article 3

For the purposes of this Directive the principle of equal treatment implies the absence of all discrimination on grounds of sex, either directly or indirectly, by reference in particular to marital or family status.

SECTION II

Equal treatment between self-employed male and female workers — position of the spouses without professional status of self-employed workers — protection of self-employed workers or wives of self-employed workers during pregnancy and motherhood

Article 4

As regards self-employed persons, Member States shall take the measures necessary to ensure the elimination of all provisions which are contrary to the principle of equal treatment as defined in Directive 76/207/EEC, especially in respect of the establishment, equipment or extension of a business or the launching or extension of any other form of self-employed activity including financial facilities.

Article 5

Without prejudice to the specific conditions for access to certain activities which apply equally to both sexes, Member States shall take the measures necessary to ensure that the conditions for the formation of a company between spouses are not more restrictive than the conditions for the formation of a company between unmarried persons.

Article 6

Where a contributory social security system for self-employed workers exists in a Member State, that Member State shall take the necessary measures to enable the spouses referred to in Article 2 (b) who are not protected under the self-employed worker's social security scheme to join a contributory social security scheme voluntarily.

Article 7

Member States shall undertake to examine under what conditions recognition of the work of the spouses referred to in Article 2 (b) may be encouraged and, in the light of such examination, consider any appropriate steps for encouraging such recognition.

Article 8

Member States shall undertake to examine whether, and under what conditions, female self-employed workers and the wives of self-employed workers may, during interruptions in their occupational activity owing to pregnancy or motherhood,

— have access to services supplying temporary replacements or existing national social services, or

— be entitled to cash benefits under a social security scheme or under any other public social protection system.

SECTION III

General and final provisions

Article 9

Member States shall introduce into their national legal systems such measures as are necessary to enable all persons who consider themselves wronged by failure to apply the principle of equal treatment in self-employed activities to pursue their claims by judicial process, possibly after recourse to other competent authorities.

Article 10

Member States shall ensure that the measures adopted pursuant to this Directive, together with the relevant provisions already in force, are brought to the attention of bodies representing self-employed workers and vocational training centres.

Article 11

The Council shall review this Directive, on a proposal from the Commission, before 1 July 1993.

Article 12

1. Member States shall bring into force the laws, regulations and administrative provisions necessary to comply with this Directive not later than 30 June 1989.

However, if a Member State which, in order to comply with Article 5 of this Directive, has to amend its legislation on matrimonial rights and obligations, the date on which such Member State must comply with Article 5 shall be 30 June 1991.

2. Member States shall immediately inform the Commission of the measures taken to comply with this Directive.

Article 13

Member States shall forward to the Commission, not later than 30 June 1991, all the information necessary to enable it to draw up a report on the application of this Directive for submission to the Council.

Article 14

This Directive is addressed to the Member States.

Done at Brussels, 11 December 1986.

For the Council
The President
A. CLARKE

COUNCIL DIRECTIVE (86/378/EEC)

of 24 July 1986

on the implementation of the principle of equal treatment for men and women in occupational social security schemes

THE COUNCIL OF THE EUROPEAN COMMUNITIES,

Having regard to the Treaty establishing the European Economic Community, and in particular Articles 100 and 235 thereof,

Having regard to the proposal from the Commission ([1]),

Having regard to the opinion of the European Parliament ([2]),

Having regard to the opinion of the Economic and Social Committee ([3]),

Whereas the Treaty provides that each Member State shall ensure the application of the principle that men and women should receive equal pay for equal work; whereas 'pay' should be taken to mean the ordinary basic or minimum wage or salary and any other consideration, whether in cash or in kind, which the worker receives, directly or indirectly, from his employer in respect of his employment;

Whereas, although the principle of equal pay does indeed apply directly in cases where discrimination can be determined solely on the basis of the criteria of equal treatment and equal pay, there are also situations in which implementation of this principle implies the adoption of additional measures which more clearly define its scope;

Whereas Article 1 (2) of Council Directive 76/207/EEC of 9 February 1976 on the implementation of the principle of equal treatment for men and women as regards access to employment, vocational training and promotion, and working conditions ([4]) provides that, with a view to ensuring the progressive implementation of the principle of equal treatment in matters of social security, the Council, acting on a proposal from the Commission, will adopt provisions defining its substance, its scope and the arrangements for its application; whereas the Council adopted to this end Directive 79/7/EEC of 19 December 1978 on the progressive implementation of the principle of equal treatment for men and women in matters of social security ([5]);

Whereas Article 3 (3) of Directive 79/7/EEC provides that, with a view to ensuring implementation of the principle of equal treatment in occupational schemes, the Council, acting on a proposal from the Commission, will adopt provisions defining its substance, its scope and the arrangements for its application;

Whereas the principle of equal treatment should be implemented in occupational social security schemes which provide protection against the risks specified in Article 3 (1) of Directive 79/7/EEC as well as those which provide employees with any other consideration in cash or in kind within the meaning of the Treaty;

Whereas implementation of the principle of equal treatment does not prejudice the provisions relating to the protection of women by reason of maternity,

HAS ADOPTED THIS DIRECTIVE:

Article 1

The object of this Directive is to implement, in occupational social security schemes, the principle of equal treatment for men and women, hereinafter referred to as 'the principle of equal treatment'.

Article 2

1. 'Occupational social security schemes' means schemes not governed by Directive 79/7/EEC whose purpose is to provide workers, whether employees or self-employed, in an undertaking or group of undertakings, area of economic activity or occupational sector or group of such sectors with benefits intended to supplement the benefits provided by statutory social security schemes or to replace them, whether membership of such schemes is compulsory or optional.

2. This Directive does not apply to:

(a) individual contracts,

(b) schemes having only one member,

(c) in the case of salaried workers, insurance schemes offered to participants individually to guarantee them:

— either additional benefits, or

— a choice of date on which the normal benefits will start, or a choice between several benefits.

([1]) OJ C 134, 21.5.1983, p. 7.
([2]) OJ C 117, 30.4.1984, p. 169.
([3]) OJ C 35, 9.2.1984, p. 7.
([4]) OJ L 39, 14.2.1976, p. 40.
([5]) OJ L 6, 10.1.1979, p. 24.

Article 3

This Directive shall apply to members of the working population including self-employed persons, persons whose activity is interrupted by illness, maternity, accident or involuntary unemployment and persons seeking employment, and to retired and disabled workers.

Article 4

This Directive shall apply to:

(a) occupational schemes which provide protection against the following risks:

— sickness,

— invalidity,

— old age, including early retirement,

— industrial accidents and occupational diseases,

— unemployment;

(b) occupational schemes which provide for other social benefits, in cash or in kind, and in particular survivors' benefits and family allowances, if such benefits are accorded to employed persons and thus constitute a consideration paid by the employer to the worker by reason of the latter's employment.

Article 5

1. Under the conditions laid down in the following provisions, the principle of equal treatment implies that there shall be no discrimination on the basis of sex, either directly or indirectly, by reference in particular to marital or family status, especially as regards:

— the scope of the schemes and the conditions of access to them;

— the obligation to contribute and the calculation of contributions;

— the calculation of benefits, including supplementary benefits due in respect of a spouse or dependants, and the conditions governing the duration and retention of entitlement to benefits.

2. The principle of equal treatment shall not prejudice the provisions relating to the protection of women by reason of maternity.

Article 6

1. Provisions contrary to the principle of equal treatment shall include those based on sex, either directly or indirectly, in particular by reference to marital or family status for:

(a) determining the persons who may participate in an occupational scheme;

(b) fixing the compulsory or optional nature of participation in an occupational scheme;

(c) laying down different rules as regards the age of entry into the scheme or the minimum period of employment or membership of the scheme required to obtain the benefits thereof;

(d) laying down different rules, except as provided for in subparagraphs (h) and (i), for the reimbursement of contributions where a worker leaves a scheme without having fulfilled the conditions guaranteeing him a deferred right to long-term benefits;

(e) setting different conditions for the granting of benefits of restricting such benefits to workers of one or other of the sexes;

(f) fixing different retirement ages;

(g) suspending the retention or acquisition of rights during periods of maternity leave or leave for family reasons which are granted by law or agreement and are paid by the employer;

(h) setting different levels of benefit, except insofar as may be necessary to take account of actuarial calculation factors which differ according to sex in the case of benefits designated as contribution-defined;

(i) setting different levels of worker contribution;

setting different levels of employer contribution in the case of benefits designated as contribution-defined, except with a view to making the amount of those benefits more nearly equal;

(j) laying down different standards or standards applicable only to workers of a specified sex, except as provided for in subparagraphs (h) and (i), as regards the guarantee or retention of entitlement to deferred benefits when a worker leaves a scheme.

2. Where the granting of benefits within the scope of this Directive is left to the discretion of the scheme's management bodies, the latter must take account of the principle of equal treatment.

Article 7

Member States shall take all necessary steps to ensure that:

(a) provisions contrary to the principle of equal treatment in legally compulsory collective agreements, staff rules of undertakings or any other arrangements relating to occupational schemes are null and void, or may be declared null and void or amended;

(b) schemes containing such provisions may not be approved or extended by administrative measures.

Article 8

1.   Member States shall take all necessary steps to ensure that the provisions of occupational schemes contrary to the principle of equal treatment are revised by 1 January 1993.

2.   This Directive shall not preclude rights and obligations relating to a period of membership of an occupational scheme prior to revision of that scheme from remaining subject to the provisions of the scheme in force during that period.

Article 9

Member States may defer compulsory application of the principle of equal treatment with regard to:

(a) determination of pensionable age for the purposes of granting old-age or retirement pensions, and the possible implications for other benefits:

   — either until the date on which such equality is achieved in statutory schemes,

   — or, at the latest, until such equality is required by a directive.

(b) survivors' pensions until a directive requires the principle of equal treatment in statutory social security schemes in that regard;

(c) the application of the first subparagraph of Article 6 (1) (i) to take account of the different actuarial calculation factors, at the latest until the expiry of a thirteen-year period as from the notification of this Directive.

Article 10

Member States shall introduce into their national legal systems such measures as are necessary to enable all persons who consider themselves injured by failure to apply the principle of equal treatment to pursue their claims before the courts, possibly after bringing the matters before other competent authorities.

Article 11

Member States shall take all the necessary steps to protect workers against dismissal where this constitutes a response on the part of the employer to a complaint made at undertaking level or to the institution of legal proceedings aimed at enforcing compliance with the principle of equal treatment.

Article 12

1.   Member States shall bring into force such laws, regulations and administrative provisions as are necessary in order to comply with this Directive at the latest three years after notification thereof (¹). They shall immediately inform the Commission thereof.

2.   Member States shall communicate to the Commission at the latest five years after notification of this Directive all information necessary to enable the Commission to draw up a report on the application of this Directive for submission to the Council.

Article 13

This Directive is addressed to the Member States.

Done at Brussels, 24 July 1986.

For the Council
The President
A. CLARK

(¹) This Directive was notified to the Member States on 30 July 1986

COUNCIL DIRECTIVE (79/7/EEC)

of 19 December 1978

on the progressive implementation of the principle of equal treatment for men and women in matters of social security

THE COUNCIL OF THE EUROPEAN COMMUNITIES,

Having regard to the Treaty establishing the European Economic Community, and in particular Article 235 thereof,

Having regard to the proposal from the Commission [1],

Having regard to the opinion of the European Parliament [2],

Having regard to the opinion of the Economic and Social Committee [3],

Whereas Article 1 (2) of Council Directive 76/207/ EEC of 9 February 1976 on the implementation of the principle of equal treatment for men and women as regards access to employment, vocational training and promotion, and working conditions [4] provides that, with a view to ensuring the progressive implementation of the principle of equal treatment in matters of social security, the Council, acting on a proposal from the Commission, will adopt provisions defining its substance, its scope and the arrangements for its application; whereas the Treaty does not confer the specific powers required for this purpose;

Whereas the principle of equal treatment in matters of social security should be implemented in the first place in the statutory schemes which provide protection against the risks of sickness, invalidity, old age, accidents at work, occupational diseases and unemployment, and in social assistance in so far as it is intended to supplement or replace the abovementioned schemes;

Whereas the implementation of the principle of equal treatment in matters of social security does not prejudice the provisions relating to the protection of women on the ground of maternity; whereas, in this respect, Member States may adopt specific provisions for women to remove existing instances of unequal treatment,

[1] OJ C 34, 11.2.1977, p. 3.
[2] OJ C 299, 12.12.1977, p. 13.
[3] OJ C 180, 28.7.1977, p. 36.
[4] OJ L 39, 14.2.1976, p. 40.

HAS ADOPTED THIS DIRECTIVE:

Article 1

The purpose of this Directive is the progressive implementation, in the field of social security and other elements of social protection provided for in Article 3, of the principle of equal treatment for men and women in matters of social security, hereinafter referred to as 'the principle of equal treatment'.

Article 2

This Directive shall apply to the working population — including self-employed persons, workers and self-employed persons whose activity is interrupted by illness, accident or involuntary unemployment and persons seeking employment — and to retired or invalided workers and self-employed persons.

Article 3

1.   This Directive shall apply to:

(a) statutory schemes which provide protection against the following risks:

— sickness,

— invalidity,

— old age,

— accidents at work and occupational diseases,

— unemployment;

(b) social assistance, in so far as it is intended to supplement or replace the schemes referred to in (a).

2.   This Directive shall not apply to the provisions concerning survivors' benefits nor to those concerning family benefits, except in the case of family benefits granted by way of increases of benefits due in respect of the risks referred to in paragraph 1 (a).

3.   With a view to ensuring implementation of the principle of equal treatment in occupational schemes, the Council, acting on a proposal from the Commission, will adopt provisions defining its substance, its scope and the arrangements for its application.

Article 4

1.　The principle of equal treatment means that there shall be no discrimination whatsoever on grounds of sex either directly, or indirectly by reference in particular to marital or family status, in particular as concerns:

— the scope of the schemes and the conditions of access thereto,

— the obligation to contribute and the calculation of contributions,

— the calculation of benefits including increases due in respect of a spouse and for dependants and the conditions governing the duration and retention of entitlement to benefits.

2.　The principle of equal treatment shall be without prejudice to the provisions relating to the protection of women on the grounds of maternity.

Article 5

Member States shall take the measures necessary to ensure that any laws, regulations and administrative provisions contrary to the principle of equal treatment are abolished.

Article 6

Member States shall introduce into their national legal systems such measures as are necessary to enable all persons who consider themselves wronged by failure to apply the principle of equal treatment to pursue their claims by judicial process, possibly after recourse to other competent authorities.

Article 7

1.　This Directive shall be without prejudice to the right of Member States to exclude from its scope:

(a) the determination of pensionable age for the purposes of granting old-age and retirement pensions and the possible consequences thereof for other benefits;

(b) advantages in respect of old-age pension schemes granted to persons who have brought up children; the acquisition of benefit entitlements following periods of interruption of employment due to the bringing up of children;

(c) the granting of old-age or invalidity benefit entitlements by virtue of the derived entitlements of a wife;

(d) the granting of increases of long-term invalidity, old-age, accidents at work and occupational disease benefits for a dependent wife;

(e) the consequences of the exercise, before the adoption of this Directive, of a right of option not to acquire rights or incur obligations under a statutory scheme.

2.　Member States shall periodically examine matters excluded under paragraph 1 in order to ascertain, in the light of social developments in the matter concerned, whether there is justification for maintaining the exclusions concerned.

Article 8

1.　Member States shall bring into force the laws, regulations and administrative provisions necessary to comply with this Directive within six years of its notification. They shall immediately inform the Commission thereof.

2.　Member States shall communicate to the Commission the text of laws, regulations and administrative provisions which they adopt in the field covered by this Directive, including measures adopted pursuant to Article 7 (2).

They shall inform the Commission of their reasons for maintaining any existing provisions on the matters referred to in Article 7 (1) and of the possibilities for reviewing them at a later date.

Article 9

Within seven years of notification of this Directive, Member States shall forward all information necessary to the Commission to enable it to draw up a report on the application of this Directive for submission to the Council and to propose such further measures as may be required for the implementation of the principle of equal treatment.

Article 10

This Directive is addressed to the Member States.

Done at Brussels, 19 December 1978.

For the Council
The President
H.-D.　GENSCHER

COUNCIL DIRECTIVE (76/207/EEC)

of 9 February 1976

on the implementation of the principle of equal treatment for men and women as regards access to employment, vocational training and promotion, and working conditions

THE COUNCIL OF THE EUROPEAN COMMUNITIES,

Having regard to the Treaty establishing the European Economic Community, and in particular Article 235 thereof,

Having regard to the proposal from the Commission,

Having regard to the opinion of the European Parliament([1]),

Having regard to the opinion of the Economic and Social Committee([2]),

Whereas the Council, in its resolution of 21 January 1974 concerning a social action programme([3]), included among the priorities action for the purpose of achieving equality between men and women as regards access to employment and vocational training and promotion and as regards working conditions, including pay;

Whereas, with regard to pay, the Council adopted on 10 February 1975 Directive 75/117/EEC on the approximation of the laws of the Member States relating to the application of the principle of equal pay for men and women([4]);

Whereas Community action to achieve the principle of equal treatment for men and women in respect of access to employment and vocational training and promotion and in respect of other working conditions also appears to be necessary; whereas, equal treatment for male and female workers constitutes one of the objectives of the Community, in so far as the harmonisation of living and working conditions while maintaining their improvement are *inter alia* to be furthered; whereas the Treaty does not confer the necessary specific powers for this purpose;

Whereas the definition and progressive implementation of the principle of equal treatment in matters of social security should be ensured by means of subsequent instruments,

HAS ADOPTED THIS DIRECTIVE:

Article 1

1.   The purpose of this Directive is to put into effect in the Member States the principle of equal treatment for men and women as regards access to employment, including promotion, and to vocational training and as regards working conditions and, on the conditions referred to in paragraph 2, social security. This principle is herinafter referred to as 'the principle of equal treatment.'

2.   With a view to ensuring the progressive implementation of the principle of equal treatment in matters of social security, the Council, acting on a proposal from the Commission, will adopt provisions defining its substance, its scope and the arrangements for its application.

Article 2

1.   For the purposes of the following provisions, the principle of equal treatment shall mean that there shall be no discrimination whatsover on grounds of sex either directly or indirectly by reference in particular to marital or family status.

2.   This Directive shall be without prejudice to the right of Member States to exclude from its field of application those occupational activities and, where appropriate, the training leading thereto, for which, by reason of their nature or the context in which they are carried out, the sex of the worker constitutes a determining factor.

3.   This Directive shall be without prejudice to provisions concerning the protection of women, particularly as regards pregnancy and maternity.

4.   This Directive shall be without prejudice to measures to promote equal opportunity for men and women, in particular by removing existing inequalities which affect women's opportunities in the areas referred to in Article 1 (1).

Article 3

1.   Application of the principle of equal treatment means that there shall be no discrimination whatsover on grounds of sex in the conditions, including selection

---

([1])   OJ C 111, 20.5.1975, p. 14.
([2])   OJ C 286, 15.12.1975, p. 8.
([3])   OJ C 13, 12.2.1974, p. 1.
([4])   OJ L 45, 19.2.1975, p. 19.

criteria, for access to all jobs or posts, whatever the sector or branch of activity, and to all levels of the occupational hierarchy.

2.   To this end, Member States shall take the measures necessary to ensure that:

(a) any laws, regulations and administrative provisions contrary to the principle of equal treatment shall be abolished;

(b) any provisions contrary to the principle of equal treatment which are included in collective agreements, individual contracts of employment, internal rules of undertakings or in rules governing the independent occupations and professions shall be, or may be declared, null and void or may be amended;

(c) those laws, regulations and administrative provisions contrary to the principle of equal treatment when the concern for protection which originally inspired them is no longer well founded shall be revised; and that where similar provisions are included in collective agreements labour and management shall be requested to undertake the desired revision.

Article 4

Application of the principle of equal treatment with regard to access to all types and to all levels, of vocational guidance, vocational training, advanced vocational training and retraining, means that Member States shall take all necessary measures to ensure that:

(a) any laws, regulations and administrative provisions contrary to the principle of equal treatment shall be abolished;

(b) any provisions contrary to the principle of equal treatment which are included in collective agreements, individual contracts of employment, internal rules of undertakings or in rules governing the independent occupations and professions shall be, or may be declared, null and void or may be amended;

(c) without prejudice to the freedom granted in certain Member States to certain private training establishments, vocational guidance, vocational training, advanced vocational training and retraining shall be accessible on the basis of the same criteria and at the same levels without any discrimination on grounds of sex.

Article 5

1.   Application of the principle of equal treatment with regard to working conditions, including the conditions governing dismissal, means that men and

women shall be guaranteed the same conditions without discrimination on grounds of sex.

2.   To this end, Member States shall take the measures necessary to ensure that:

(a) any laws, regulations and administrative provisions contrary to the principle of equal treatment shall be abolished;

(b) any provisions contrary to the principle of equal treatment which are included in collective agreements, individual contracts of employment, internal rules of undertakings or in rules governing the independent occupations and professions shall be, or may be declared, null and void or may be amended;

(c) those laws, regulations and administrative provisions contrary to the principle of equal treatment when the concern for protection which originally inspired them is no longer well founded shall be revised; and that where similar provisions are included in collective agreements labour and management shall be requested to undertake the desired revision.

Article 6

Member States shall introduce into their national legal systems such measures as are necessary to enable all persons who consider themselves wronged by failure to apply to them the principle of equal treatment within the meaning of Articles 3, 4 and 5 to pursue their claims by judicial process after possible recourse to other competent authorities.

Article 7

Member States shall take the necessary measures to protect employees against dismissal by the employer as a reaction to a complaint within the undertaking or to any legal proceedings aimed at enforcing compliance with the principle of equal treatment.

Article 8

Member States shall take care that the provisions adopted pursuant to this Directive, together with the relevant provisions already in force, are brought to the attention of employees by all appropriate means, for example at their place of employment.

Article 9

1.   Member States shall put into force the laws, regulations and administrative provisions necessary in order to comply with this Directive within 30 months

of its notification and shall immediately inform the Commission thereof.

However, as regards the first part of Article 3 (2) (c) and the first part of Article 5 (2) (c), Member States shall carry out a first examination and if necessary a first revision of the laws, regulations and administrative provisions referred to therein within four years of notification of this Directive.

2. Member States shall periodically assess the occupational activities referred to in Article 2 (2) in order to decide, in the light of social developments, whether there is justification for maintaining the exclusions concerned. They shall notify the Commission of the results of this assessment.

3. Member States shall also communicate to the Commission the texts of laws, regulations and administrative provisions which they adopt in the field covered by this Directive.

Article 10

Within two years following expiry of the 30-month period laid down in the first subparagraph of Article 9 (1), Member States shall forward all necessary information to the Commission to enable it to draw up a report on the application of this Directive for submission to the Council.

Article 11

This Directive is addressed to the Member States.

Done at Brussels, 9 February 1976.

For the Council
The President
G. THORN

COUNCIL DIRECTIVE (75/117/EEC)

of 10 February 1975

on the approximation of the laws of the Member States relating to the application of the principle of equal pay for men and women

THE COUNCIL OF THE EUROPEAN COMMUNITIES,

Having regard to the Treaty establishing the European Economic Community, and in particular Article 100 thereof;

Having regard to the proposal from the Commission;

Having regard to the opinion of the European Parliament [1];

Having regard to the opinion of the Economic and Social Committee [2];

Whereas implementation of the principle that men and women should receive equal pay contained in Article 119 of the Treaty is an integral part of the establishment and functioning of the common market;

Whereas it is primarily the responsibility of the Member States to ensure the application of this principle by means of appropriate laws, regulations and administrative provisions;

Whereas the Council resolution of 21 January 1974 [3] concerning a social action programme, aimed at making it possible to harmonise living and working conditions while the improvement is being maintained and at achieving a balanced social and economic development of the Community, recognised that priority should be given to action taken on behalf of women as regards access to employment and vocational training and advancement, and as regards working conditions, including pay;

Whereas it is desirable to reinforce the basic laws by standards aimed at facilitating the pratical application of the principle of equality in such a way that all employees in the Community can be protected in these matters;

Whereas differences continue to exist in the various Member States despite the efforts made to apply the resolution of the conference of the Member States of 30 December 1961 on equal pay for men and women and whereas, therefore, the national provisions should be approximated as regards application of the principle of equal pay,

---

[1] OJ C 55, 13.5.1974, p. 43.
[2] OJ C 88, 26.7.1974, p. 7.
[3] OJ C 13. 12.2.1974, p. 1.

HAS ADOPTED THIS DIRECTIVE:

Article 1

The principle of equal pay for men and women outlined in Article 119 of the Treaty, hereinafter called 'principle of equal pay', means, for the same work or for work to which equal value is attributed, the elimination of all discrimination on grounds of sex with regard to all aspects and conditions of remuneration.

In particular, where a job classification system is used for determining pay, it must be based on the same criteria for both men and women and so drawn up as to exclude any discrimination on grounds of sex.

Article 2

Member States shall introduce into their national legal systems such measures as are necessary to enable all employees who consider themselves wronged by failure to apply the principle of equal pay to pursue their claims by judicial process after possible recourse to other competent authorities.

Article 3

Member States shall abolish all discrimination between men and women arising from laws, regulations or administrative provisions which is contrary to the principle of equal pay.

Article 4

Member States shall take the necessary measures to ensure that provisions appearing in collective agreements, wage scales, wage agreements or individual contracts of employment which are contrary to the principle of equal pay shall be, or may be declared, null and void or may be amended.

Article 5

Member States shall take the necessary measures to protect employees against dismissal by the employer as a reaction to a complaint within the undertaking or to any legal proceedings aimed at enforcing compliance with the principle of equal pay.

Article 6

Member States shall, in accordance with their national circumstances and legal systems, take the measures necessary to ensure that the principle of equal pay is applied. They shall see that effective means are available to take care that this principle is observed.

Article 7

Member States shall take care that the provisions adopted pursuant to this Directive, together with the relevant provisions already in force, are brought to the attention of employees by all appropriate means, for example at their place of employment.

Article 8

1.   Member States shall put into force the laws, regulations and administrative provisions necessary in order to comply with this Directive within one year of its notification and shall immediately inform the Commission thereof.

2.   Member States shall communicate to the Commission the texts of the laws, regulations and administrative provisions which they adopt in the field covered by this Directive.

Article 9

Within two years of the expiry of the one-year period referred to in Article 8, Member States shall forward all necessary information to the Commission to enable it to draw up a report on the application of this Directive for submission to the Council.

Article 10

This Directive is addressed to the Member States.

Done at Brussels, 10 February 1975.

For the Council
The President
G. FITZGERALD

Council decision

COUNCIL DECISION (95/593/EC)

of 22 December 1995

on a medium-term Community action programme on equal opportunities for men and women (1996 to 2000)

THE COUNCIL OF THE EUROPEAN UNION,

Having regard to the Treaty establishing the European Community, and in particular Article 235 thereof,

Having regard to the proposal from the Commission[1],

Having regard to the opinion of the European Parliament[2],

Having regard to the opinion of the Economic and Social Committee[3],

1. Whereas the Council has adopted six Directives, two recommendations and 10 resolutions in the area of equal treatment and equal opportunities for men and women[4];

2. Whereas these Directives and acts have played a major part in improving the situation of women;

3. Whereas equal treatment and equal opportunities for men and women are basic principles recognised by Community law;

4. Whereas the Heads of State or Government meeting within the European Council on 10 and 11 December 1994 at Essen and on 26 and 27 June 1995 at Cannes emphasised that equal opportunities for men and women, and the fight against unemployment, are the priority tasks of the European Union and its Member States;

5. Whereas, in their resolution of 6 December 1994 on equal participation by women in an employment-intensive economic growth strategy within the European Union[5], the Council and the Representatives of the Governments of the Member States meeting within the Council put various requests to the Commission in preparation for the fourth action programme on equal opportunities for men and women (1996 to 2000);

6. Whereas the said programme is in line with the aims set out in the conclusions of the World Conference on Women in Beijing;

7. Whereas in the White Paper on Growth, Competitiveness, Employment, the Commission underlines the need to strengthen equal opportunities policies for men and women in employment;

8. Whereas, in the White Paper on European Social Policy, the Commission undertook to present during 1995 a fourth action programme on equal

---

[1] OJ C 306, 17.11.1995, p. 2.

[2] OJ C 323, 4.12.1995.

[3] Opinion delivered on 22 November 1995 (not yet published in the Official Journal).

[4] Council Directive 75/117/EEC of 10 February 1975 on the approximation of the laws of the Member States relating to the application of the principle of equal pay for men and women (OJ L 45, 19.2.1975, p. 19).
Council Directive 76/207/EEC of 9 February 1976 on the implementation of the principle of equal treatment for men and women as regards access to employment, vocational training and promotion, and working conditions (OJ L 39, 14.2.1976, p. 40).
Council Directive 79/7/EEC of 19 December 1978 on the progressive implementation of the principle of equal treatment for men and women in matters of social security (OJ L 6, 10.1.1979, p. 24).
Council Directive 86/378/EEC of 24 July 1986 on the implementation of the principle of equal treatment for men and women in occupational social security schemes (OJ L 225, 12.8.1986, p. 40).
Council Directive 86/313/EEC of 11 December 1986 on the application of the principle of equal treatment between men and women engaged in an activity, including agriculture, in a self-employed capacity, and on the protection of self-employed women during pregnancy and motherhood (OJ L 359, 19.12.1986, p. 56).

Council Directive 92/85/EEC of 19 October 1992 on the introduction of measures to encourage improvements in the safety and health at work of pregnant workers and workers who have recently given birth or are breastfeeding (OJ L 348, 28.11.1992, p. 1).
Council Recommendation 84/635/EEC of 13 December 1984 on the promotion of positive action for women (OJ L 331, 19.12.1984, p. 34).
Council Recommendation 92/241/EEC of 31 March 1992 on child care (OJ L 123, 8.5.1992, p. 16).
Council resolution of 12 July 1982 on the promotion of equal opportunities for women (OJ C 186, 21.7.1982, p. 3).
Council resolution of 7 June 1984 on the action to combat unemployment amongst women (OJ C 161, 21.6.1984, p. 4).
Resolution of the Council and the Ministers for Education meeting within the Council of 3 June 1985 containing an action programme on equal opportunities for girls and boys in education (OJ C 166, 5.7.1985, p. 1).
Second Council resolution of 24 July 1986 on the promotion of equal opportunities for women (OJ C 203, 12.8.1986, p. 2).
Council resolution of 16 December 1988 on the reintegration and late integration of women into working life (OJ C 333, 28.12.1988, p. 1).
Council resolution of 29 May 1990 on the protection of the dignity of women and men at work (OJ C 157, 27.6.1990, p. 3).
Council resolution of 21 May 1991 on the third medium-term Community action programme on equal opportunities for women and men (1991 to 1995) (OJ C 142, 31.5.1991, p. 1).
Council resolution of 22 June 1994 on the promotion of equal opportunities for women and men through action by the European Structural Funds (OJ C 231, 20.8.1994, p. 1).
Resolution of the Council and of the Representatives of the Governments of the Member States meeting within the Council of 6 December 1994 on equal participation by women in an employment-intensive economic growth strategy within the European Union (OJ C 368, 23.12.1994, p. 3).
Council Resolution of 27 March 1995 on the balanced participation of women and men in decision-making (OJ C 168, 4.7.1995, p. 3)

[5] OJ C 368, 23.12.1994, p. 3.

opportunities for men and women, to come into force in 1996;

9. Whereas the European Parliament has strongly and repeatedly urged the European Union to strengthen its policy in the field of equal treatment and equal opportunities for men and women;

10. Whereas the first three medium-term Community action programmes on equal opportunities for men and women (1982 to 1985, 1986 to 1990, 1991 to 1995) have played an important role in improving the situation of women and in promoting cooperation at all levels in this area;

11. Whereas it is necessary to consolidate and build upon the results of the three programmes; whereas, despite the efforts made at both national and Community level, inequalities continue to exist, particularly with regard to the employment and pay of women;

12. Whereas the European Union's Information Offices in the Member States should step up their efforts to disseminate information on the Community's equal treatment and equal opportunities policies for men and women;

13. Whereas developing education and vocational training, diversifying the choice of jobs available and increasing the number of working women can help enhance the competitiveness of the European economy and improve integration into the labour market;

14. Whereas there is a need to develop measures taking into account economic and social change and, in particular, to respond to changes in family structures, in the roles of women and men in society, in the organisation of working life and in the demographic composition of society;

15. Whereas active partnership between the Commission, the Member States, the social partners, non-governmental organisations and in particular women's organisations needs to be promoted in this area and synergy between all the relevant policies and measures encouraged;

16. Whereas the present programme can, in accordance with Article 3b of the Treaty and having regard to the responsibility of the Member States for promoting equal treatment and equal opportunities for men and women, bring added value by identifying and stimulating good practice and policies, encouraging innovation and exchanging relevant experience, including in the field of positive actions;

17. Whereas the present programme is not intended to support all measures in favour of women

which can be undertaken locally and may, in some cases, receive aid from other Community policies;

18. Whereas the Commission has submitted, together with the proposal for this Decision, a fourth medium-term Community action programme on equal opportunities for men and women;

19. Whereas a financial reference amount, within the meaning of point 2 of the declaration by the European Parliament, the Council and the Commission of 6 March 1995, is included in this Decision for the entire duration of the programme, without thereby affecting the powers of the budgetary authority as they are defined by the Treaty;

20. Whereas the Treaty does not provide, for the adopting of this Decision, powers other than those of Article 235,

HAS DECIDED AS FOLLOWS:

Article 1

Establishment of a Community action programme

This Decision establishes a medium-term Community action programme on equal opportunities for men and women, hereinafter referred to as 'the programme', for the period from 1 January 1996 to 31 December 2000.

Article 2

Principle of integrating the equal opportunities for men and women dimension in all policies and activities (mainstreaming)

The programme is intended to promote the integration of equal opportunities for men and women in the process of preparing, implementing and monitoring all policies and activities of the European Union and the Member States, having regard to their respective powers.

Article 3

Aims

1. The programme shall support Member States' efforts in the area of equal opportunities for men and women.

2. The programme has the following aims:

(a) to promote integration of the equal opportunities for men and women dimension in all policies and activities;

(b) to mobilise all the actors in economic and social life to achieve equal opportunities for men and women;

(c) to promote equal opportunities for men and women in a changing economy, especially in the fields of education, vocational training and the labour market;

(d) to reconcile working and family life for men and women;

(e) to promote a gender balance in decision-making;

(f) to make conditions more conducive to exercising equality rights.

Article 4

Community actions

1. With a view to achieving the aims set out in Article 3, the following actions shall be implemented, enhanced and/or supported under the programme using existing structures, improving their operation and/or rationalising them where necessary:

(a) in order to allow the exchange of information and experience on good practice, methodological and/or technical and/or financial support for projects to identify and develop good practice and transfer information and experience thereon;

(b) observing and monitoring relevant policies and conducting studies in this field;

(c) rapid dissemination of the results of the initiatives embarked upon and any other relevant information.

2. The provisions regarding the criteria for applying this Article are set out in the Annex.

Article 5

Consistency and complementarity

The Commission and the Member States shall ensure consistency and complementary between the initiatives undertaken under the programme and under the Structural Funds and other Community policies or activities, including those relating to education and vocational training, and those pursued by the Member States.

Article 6

Participation of other countries

1. The programme activities which may be opened up to the participation of the countries of the European Economic Area, the associated countries of central and eastern Europe (ACCEE), Cyprus and Malta and the European Union's partner countries in the Mediterranean shall be defined in the context of the European Union's relations with those countries.

2. The cost of the participation referred to in paragraph 1 shall be covered either by the countries concerned out of their own budgets or by Community budget headings relating to the implementation of the cooperation, association or partnership agreements with these countries in the area concerned.

Article 7

Implementation

The Commission shall, in consultation with the Member States, implement the programme in accordance with this Decision.

Article 8

Determination of financial assistance

1. For the actions referred to in Article 4 (1) (a), the Community's financial contribution may amount to:

— as a general rule, a maximum of 60 %;

— in exceptional cases, in accordance with criteria established following the procedure laid down in Article 9, a higher maximum rate.

2. The actions referred to in Article 4 (1) (b) and (c) shall be financed entirely by the Community.

Article 9

Committee

1. The Commission shall be assisted by a committee composed of representatives of the Member States and chaired by a representative of Commission.

2. The following shall be adopted in accordance with the procedure referred to in paragraph 3:

— the general guidelines for the support to be supplied by the Community;

— the annual work programme and matters relating to the internal breakdown of the programme;

— procedures for the selection of the actions supported by the Community, the criteria for the follow-up and evaluation of these actions and of the programme as a whole, and the arrangements for the dissemination and transfer of results.

3. The representative of the Commission shall submit to the committee a draft of the measures to be

taken. The committee shall deliver its opinion on the draft within a time limit which the chairman may lay down according to the urgency of the matter. The opinion shall be delivered by the majority laid down in Article 148 (2) of the Treaty in the case of decisions which the Council is required to adopt on a proposal from the Commission. The votes of the representatives of the Member States within the committee shall be weighted in the manner set out in that Article. The chairman shall not vote.

The Commission shall adopt measures which apply immediately. However, if these measures are not in accordance with the opinion of the committee, they shall be communicated by the Commission to the Council forthwith.

In that event, the Commission shall defer application of the measures which it has decided for a period of two months from the date of such communication.

The Council, acting by a qualified majority, may take a different decision within the time limit referred to in the previous subparagraph.

Article 10

Financing

1.   The financial reference amount for the implementation of the programme for the period 1 January 1996 to 31 December 2000 shall be ECU 30 million.

2.   The annual appropriations shall be authorised by the budgetary authority within the limits of the financial perspective.

Article 11

Monitoring and evaluation

1.   The actions supported by the programme shall be continuously monitored with a view to ensuring their effectiveness in accordance with the criteria established following the procedure referred to in Article 9.

2.   The programme shall be subject to regular objective external evaluations in accordance with criteria laid down following the procedure referred to in Article 9.

Article 12

Reports

1.   The Commission shall submit an interim report on the implementation of the programme to the European Parliament, the Council, the Economic and Social Committee and the Committee of the Regions by 31 December 1998 at the latest.

2.   The Commission shall submit a final report on the implementation of the programme to the European Parliament, the Council, the Economic and Social Committee and the Committee of the Regions by 31 December 2001 at the latest.

Article 13

This Decision shall be published in the *Official Journal of the European Communities*.

Done at Brussels, 22 December 1995.

For the Council
The President
L. ATIENZA SERNA

PROVISIONS RELATING TO THE CRITERIA FOR APPLYING ARTICLE 4

I. INTRODUCTORY COMMENTS

The programme is intended to support efforts to promote equal opportunities for men and women at European Union, national, regional and local levels, having full regard to their respective powers.

The programme constitutes a significant addition to the action undertaken within the framework of other Community policies, including the Structural Funds. Accordingly, the programme is not intended to support all measures in favour of women which can be undertaken locally and may, in some cases, receive aid from those policies.

The added value of the programme lies in the identification and exchange of information and experience on good practice in the field of equal opportunities for men and women.

II. AREAS OF ACTION

Community actions which may receive support under the programme are those referred to in Article 4 and must concern one or more of the following areas:

1. **Integration of the equal opportunities for men and women dimension in all policies and activities (mainstreaming):**

   — promotion and development of methods, strategies, models and studies aimed at integrating the equal opportunities dimension in all policies and activities.

2. **Employment and working life:**

   — education, training and continuing training and the promotion of equal opportunities for men and women in employment,

   — access to employment and conditions of employment,

   — promotion of economic independence,

   — vertical and horizontal desegregation of the labour market,

   — equal pay for equal work and work of equal value,

   — organisation and flexibility of working life,

   — aspects linked with the working environment, including sexual harassment,

   — entrepreneurism,

   — reconciliation of professional and parental responsibilities, including the role of men.

3. **Decision-making:**

   — development and monitoring of methods, strategies and actions to promote balanced participation of men and women in decision-making, including in senior posts.

4. **Information and research:**

   — promotion of information, research, studies and other actions to increase knowledge and promote favourable attitudes to equal opportunities for men and women.

5. Statistics:

— better use and development of statistics broken down according to gender, in consultation with the competent national bodies.

III. SELECTION CRITERIA

1. To qualify for support under the programme, actions must meet the following criteria:

    — present added value at European Union level,

    — aim to promote best practice in the area(s) concerned,

    — contribute to one or more of the aims set out in Article 3,

    — permit transitional exchanges,

    — target transferable results,

    — be submitted and implemented by public and private parties and organisations which have appropriate qualifications and/or experience,

    — have clear and precise objectives and have a realistic time span give those objectives,

    — be evaluated objectively and regularly.

2. With regard to the actions referred to in Article 4 (1) (a), priority will be given to actions which meet one or more of the following criteria:

    — make provision, where appropriate, for the participation of more than one partner, in particular the social partners, non-governmental organisations and especially women's organisations and local authorities,

    — involve practical measures aimed at promoting equal opportunities for men and women in the above areas,

    — be innovatory, as far as possible, in terms of content and organisation,

    — lend themselves to the broadest possible transfer opportunities within the European Union,

    — encourage co-financing.

IV. METHOD OF PRESENTING APPLICATIONS FOR SUPPORT

1. Applications for support under the programme must contain the following information:

    — exact particulars of the full identity of action promoters and partners,

    — detailed description of the proposed action,

    — detailed budget estimate covering the entire action and indicating all definite and/ or expected sources of financing,

    — summary of any application for financing.

2. Applications for support will be presented to the Commission and, at the same time, to the Member States concerned, for information and, where appropriate, for an opinion, in line with national practice.

———————————————

Commission
decisions

COMMISSION DECISION (95/420/EC)

of 19 July 1995

amending Decision 82/43/EEC relating to the setting up of an Advisory Committee on Equal Opportunities for Women and Men

THE COMMISSION OF THE EUROPEAN COMMUNITIES,

Having regard to the Treaty establishing the European Community,

Whereas the constant improvement of living and working conditions and the harmonious development of economies constitute objectives of the European Economic Community;

Whereas the Heads of State or Government, meeting within the European Council on 10 and 11 December 1994, emphasised that equality of opportunity for women and men, together with the fight against unemployment, is a paramount task of the European Union and its Member States;

Whereas equality between women and men is essential to human dignity and democracy, and constitutes a fundamental principle of Community law, of the constitutions and laws of the Member States, and of international and European conventions;

Whereas the application in practice of the principle of equal treatment for women and men must be encouraged by improved cooperation and exchanges of views and experience between those bodies which have special responsibility in the Member States for promoting equality of opportunity, the social partners and the Commission;

Whereas the full implementation in practice of the six Directives, two recommendations and nine resolutions adopted by the Council in the field of equal opportunities (¹) can be speeded

---

(¹) Council Directive 75/117/EEC of 10 February 1975 on the approximation of the laws of the Member States relating to the application of the principle of equal pay for men and women (OJ L 45, 19.2.1975, p. 19);
Council Directive 76/207/EEC of 9 February 1976 on the implementation of the principle of equal treatment for men and women as regards access to employment, vocational training and promotion, and working conditions (OJ L 39, 14.2.1976, p. 40);
Council Directive 79/7/EEC of 19 December 1978 on the progressive implementation of the principle of equal treatment for men and women in matters of social security (OJ L 6, 10.1.1979, p. 24);
Council Directive 86/378/EEC of 24 July 1986 on the implementation of the principle of equal treatment for men and women in occupational social security schemes (OJ L 225, 12.8.1986, p. 40);
Council Directive 86/613/EEC of 11 December 1986 on the application of the principle of equal treatment between men and women engaged in an activity, including agriculture, in a self-employed capacity, and on the protection of self-employed women during pregnancy and motherhood (OJ L 359, 19.12.1986, p. 56);
Council Directive 92/85/EEC of 19 October 1992 on the introduction of measures to encourage improvements in the safety and health at work of pregnant workers and workers who have recently given birth or are breast-feeding (OJ L 348, 28.11.1992, p. 1);
Council resolution of 12 July 1982 on the promotion of equal opportunities for women (OJ C 186, 21.7.1982, p. 3);
Council resolution of 7 June 1984 on action to combat unemployment amongst women (OJ C 161, 21.6.1984, p. 4);
Resolution of the Council and of the Ministers for Education meeting within the Council of 3 June 1985 containing an action programme on equal opportunities for girls and boys in education (OJ C 166, 5.7.1985, p. 1);
Second Council resolution of 24 July 1986 on the promotion of equal opportunities for women (OJ C 203, 12.8.1986, p. 2);
Council resolution of 16 December 1988 on the reintegration and late integration of women into working life (OJ C 333, 28.12.1988, p. 1);
Council resolution of 29 May 1990 on the protection of the dignity of women and men at work (OJ C 157, 27.6.1990, p. 3);
Council resolution of 21 May 1991 on the third medium-term Community action programme on equal opportunities for women and men (1991-95) (OJ C 142, 31.5.1991, p. 1);
Council resolution of 22 June 1994 on the promotion of equal opportunities for women and men through action by the European Structural Funds (OJ C 231, 20.8.1994, p. 1);
Council resolution of 27 March 1995 on the balanced participation of women and men in decision-making (OJ C 168, 4.7.1995, p. 3);
Council Recommendation 84/635/EEC of 13 December 1984 on the promotion of positive action for women (OJ L 331, 19.12.1984, p. 34);
Council Recommendation 92/241/EEC of 31 March 1992 on child care (OJ L 123, 8.5.1992, p. 16).

up considerably with the assistance of national bodies having a network of specialised information at their disposal;

Whereas the preparation, implementation and monitoring of the Community's activities to promote equal opportunities require close cooperation with specialised bodies in the Member States and with the social partners, thereby necessitating an institutional framework for the purpose of regular consultation with those parties;

Whereas the Advisory Committee on Equal Opportunities for Women and Men, established by Commission Decision 82/43/EEC of 9 December 1981 (¹), has made a significant contribution to the Community's activities in this field, particularly in terms of following up successive Community action programmes both through its opinions and through its cooperation, on a partnership basis, with the Commission;

Whereas the composition and terms of reference of the Committee have to be adapted to take account of current and future developments with a view to promoting equal opportunities, as outlined in the Commission communication of 19 July 1995 proposing a new medium-term action programme in this connection; whereas it is therefore necessary to amend Decision 82/43/EEC,

HAS DECIDED AS FOLLOWS:

Article 1

Decision 82/43/EEC is hereby amended as follows:

1. Articles 2 and 3 are replaced by the following text:

'*Article 2*

1.   The Committee shall assist the Commission in formulating and implementing the Community's activities aimed at promoting equal opportunities for women and men, and shall foster ongoing exchanges of relevant experience, policies and practices between the Member States and the various parties involved.

2.   To achieve the aims referred to in paragraph 1 above, the Committee shall:

(a) assist the Commission in the development of instruments for monitoring, evaluating and disseminating the results of measures taken at Union level to promote equal opportunities;

(b) contribute to the implementation of Community action programmes in the field, mainly by analysing the results and suggesting improvements to the measures taken;

(c) contribute, through its opinion, to the preparation of the Commission's annual report on progress made towards achieving equality of opportunity for women and men;

(d) encourage exchanges of information on measures taken at all levels to promote equal opportunities and, where appropriate, put forward proposals for possible follow-up action;

(e) deliver opinions or submit reports to the Commission, either at the latter's request or on its own initiative, on any matter of relevance to the promotion of equal opportunities in the Community.

3.   Procedures for the circulation of the Committee's opinions and reports shall be determined in agreement with the Commission. They may be published as an annex to the Commission's annual report on equal opportunities for women and men.

_____
(¹) OJ L 20, 28.1.1982, p. 35.

Article 3

1.   The Committee shall comprise 40 members, i.e.:

(a) one representative per Member State from ministries or government departments responsible for promoting equal opportunities; the representative shall be designated by the Government of each Member State;

(b) one representative per Member State from national committees or bodies set up by official decision, having specific responsibility for equal opportunities between women and men through representation of the sectors concerned. Where there are several committees or bodies dealing with these matters in a Member State, the Commission shall determine which body, by its objectives, structure, representativeness and degree of independence, is best qualified to be represented on the Committee. Any country without such committees shall be represented by members of bodies deemed by the Commission to perform analogous duties; the representative shall be appointed by the Commission, acting on a proposal from the relevant national committee or body;

(c) — five members representing employers' organisations at Community level;

    — five members representing workers' organisations at Community level.

The representatives shall be appointed by the Commission, acting on a proposal from the social partners at Community level.

2.   Two representatives of the European Women's Lobby shall attend meetings of the Committee as observers.

3.   Representatives of international and professional organisations and other associations making duly substantiated requests to the Commission may be given observer status.'

2.   Article 6 is replaced by the following text:

'*Article 6*

The Committee shall elect a chairperson, with a one-year term of office, from among its members. Election shall be by a majority of two-thirds of the members present; a minimum of half the total votes in favour shall, nevertheless, be required.

Two vice-chairpersons shall be elected by the same majority and under the same conditions. They shall be required to stand in for the chairperson in the absence of the latter. The chairperson and vice-chairpersons must belong to different Member States. They shall constitute the Bureau of the Committee, which shall meet before each meeting of the Committee.

The Commission shall organise the work of the Committee in close cooperation with the chairperson. The draft agenda for meetings of the Committee shall be set by the Commission in agreement with the chairperson. The Secretariat of the Committee shall be provided by the Commission's Equal Opportunities Unit. The minutes of the Committee's meetings shall be drawn up by the Commission and submitted to the Committee for approval.'

3.   A third paragraph is added to Article 8 as follows:

'3.   One or more members of the Committee may participate as observers in the activities of other advisory committees of the Commission, and shall inform the Committee accordingly.'

4. Articles 10 and 11 are replaced by the following text:

'*Article 10*

The Committee shall be convened by the Commission and shall meet on its premises. It shall meet at least twice a year.

Article 11

The Committee's deliberations deal with the requests for opinion presented by the Commission or with the opinions which the Committee delivers on its own initiative. They are not followed by a vote.

The Commission, when requesting the Committee's opinion, may set a deadline within which the opinion should be delivered.

The views expressed by the different categories represented in the Committee are recorded in the minutes, which are transmitted to the Commission.

Where the opinion requested has been agreed unanimously by the Committee, it will draft common conclusions which are annexed to the minutes.'

Article 2

This Decision shall take effect on 1 January 1996.

Done at Brussels, 19 July 1995.

For the Commission
Pádraig FLYNN
Member of the Commission

———————

COMMISSION DECISION (82/43/EEC)

of 9 December 1982

relating to the setting up of an Advisory Committee on Equal Opportunities for Women and Men

THE COMMISSION OF THE EUROPEAN COMMUNITIES,

Having regard to the Treaty establishing the European Economic Community,

Whereas the application in practice of the principle of equal treatment for women and men must be encouraged by improved cooperation and exchanges of views and experience between those bodies which have special responsibility in the Member States for promoting equality of opportunity, and the Commission;

Whereas the full implementation in practice of Council Directives 75/117/EEC of 10 February 1975 on the approximation of the laws of the Member States relating to the application of the principle of equal pay for men and women ([1]), 76/207/EEC of 9 February 1976 on the implementation of the principle of equal treatment for men and women as regards access to employment, vocational training and promotion, and working conditions ([2]) and 79/7/EEC of 19 December 1978 on the progressive implementation of the principle of equal treatment for men and women in matters of social security ([3]) will be speeded up considerably as a result of the assistance of national bodies with a network of specialised information at their disposal;

Taking account of Directive 72/161/EEC of 17 April 1972 concerning the provision of socio-economic guidance for and the acquisition of occupational skills by persons engaged in agriculture ([4]);

Whereas the preparation and implementation of Community measures concerning the employment of women, the improvement of the position of women who are self-employed and those engaged in agriculture, and the promotion of equal opportunities require close cooperation with the specialised bodies in Member States;

Whereas, therefore, an institutional framework should be set up for the purpose of regular consultations with those bodies,

---

([1]) OJ L 45, 19.2.1975, p. 19.
([2]) OJ L 39, 14.2.1976, p. 40.
([3]) OJ L 6, 10.1.1979, p. 24.
([4]) OJ L 96, 23.4.1972, p. 15.

HAS DECIDED AS FOLLOWS:

Article 1

The Commission hereby establishes an Advisory Committee on Equal Opportunities for Women and Men, hereinafter called 'the Committee'.

Article 2

1. The Committee shall advise the Commission on the formulation and implementation of its policy to promote women's employment and equal treatment and ensure the continuous exchange of information on experience gained and measures undertaken in the Community in the fields in question.

2. To achieve the aims referred to in paragraph 1 above, the Committee:

— shall exchange information with the Commission on action taken at Community and national level and where appropriate on the follow-up to be given such action,

— shall issue opinions or forward reports to the Commission, particularly in regard to the equal opportunities policy, either at the latter's request or on its own initiative, and to this end shall promote exchanges of information on experience in Member States in sectors within its competence.

3. Procedures for the circulation of the Committee's opinions and reports shall be determined in agreement with the Commission.

Article 3

1. The Committee shall have 20 members.

2. It shall be composed of two representatives from each Member State appointed from among the members of national committees or bodies set up by official decision, specifically responsible for questions of women's employment and/or equal opportunities for women and men and representing the sectors concerned. Where there are several such committees or bodies dealing with this subject in a Member State, the Commission shall determine which body, by its objectives, structure, representativeness and degree of independence is best qualified to be represented on the Committee. Any country without such a committee

shall be represented by members of bodies considered by the Commission to perform analogous duties.

3. The members of the Committee shall be appointed individually by the Commission, acting on a proposal from the bodies referred to in paragraph 2 above, from among the members of those bodies or their secretariats.

4. The representatives of the two sides of industry at Community level may attend meetings of the Committee as observers, according to the procedure to be determined by their organisations and the Commission.

Article 4

An alternate shall be appointed for each member of the Committee under the same conditions as those laid down in Article 3. Without prejudice to the provisions of Article 7, the alternate shall not attend meetings of the Committee nor participate in its work unless the relevant member is prevented from doing so.

Article 5

The term of office of members of the Committee shall be three years and shall be renewable.

At the end of the three-year period, the members of the Committee shall continue in office until a replacement is provided or their term of office is renewed.

A member's term of office shall come to an end before the expiry of the three-year period in the event of her/his resignation, the termination of her/his membership of the organisation which she/he represents, or her/his death. A member's terms of office may also be terminated if the organisation which nominated her/him requests her/his replacement.

The member shall be replaced for the remainder of the term of office in accordance with the procedure laid down in Article 4.

No remuneration shall be attachd to member's duties; travelling and subsistence expenses for meetings of the Committee and the working parties set up under Article 8 shall be met by the Commission in accordance with the administrative rules in force.

Article 6

The Committee shall elect a chairperson from among its members for a period of one year. Election shall be by a majority of two-thirds of the members present; a minimum of 10 votes in favour shall, nevertheless, be required.

The Committee shall elect two vice-chairpersons by the same majority and under the same conditions. In the absence of the chairperson, one of the vice-chairpersons shall take the chair. The chairperson and vice-chairpersons shall belong to different Member States.

The Commission shall organise the work of the Committee in close cooperation with the chairperson, and secretarial services shall be provided by the bureau for questions concerning employment and equal treatment for women of the Commission.

Article 7

The chairperson may invite any person who is specially qualified in a particular subject on the agenda to take part in its work as an expert.

Experts shall only take part in the work on the particular subject for which their attendance is requested.

Article 8

1. The Committee may set up working parties.

2. For the preparation of its opinions, the Committee may entrust a rapporteur or an outside expert with the task of drawing up reports in accordance with procedures to be determined.

Article 9

Measures adopted under Article 7 and 8 having financial implications for the budget of the European Communities shall be submitted for the prior agreement of the Commission and shall be implemented in accordance with the administrative rules in force.

Article 10

1. The Committee shall be convened by the Commission and shall meet on its premises. It shall meet at least three times a year.

2. Representatives of the Commission shall be entitled to take part in meetings of the Committee and its working parties.

Article 11

Where the Committee's deliberations are followed by a vote, a two-thirds majority of the members present shall be required. The minimum shall, however, be 10 votes in favour. Where any minority views are expressed, they shall be recorded in the minutes which shall form an Annex to the opinion.

Article 12

Without prejudice to the provisions of Article 214 of the Treaty, members of the Committee are required not to disclose information obtained in the course of their work on the Committee or its working parties when informed by the Commission that the opinion requested or question asked concerns a confidential matter.

In such cases, only members of the Committee and representatives of the Commission departments shall attend meetings.

Article 13

This Decision shall enter into force on 1 January 1982.

Done at Brussels, 9 December 1981.

For the Commission
The President
G. THORN

Council
recommendations

COUNCIL RECOMMENDATION (96/694/EC)

of 2 December 1996

on the balanced participation of women and men in the decision-making process

THE COUNCIL OF THE EUROPEAN UNION,

Having regard to the Treaty establishing the European Community, and in particular Article 235 thereof,

Having regard to the proposals from the Commission,

Having regard to the opinion of the European Parliament [1],

Having regard to the opinion of the Economic and Social Committee [2],

(1) Whereas the Council has adopted a series of legislative instruments and a number of political commitments in the field of equal treatment and equal opportunities for men and women [3] [4] [5] [6];

---

[1] OJ C 166, 10.6.1996, p. 276.

[2] OJ C 204, 15.7.1996, p. 21.

[3] — Council Directive 75/117/EEC of 10 February 1975 on the approximation of the laws of the Member States relating to the application of the principle of equal pay for men and women (OJ L 45, 19.2.1975, p. 19).
— Council Directive 76/207/EEC of 9 February 1976 on the implementation of the principle of equal treatment for men and women as regards access to employment, vocational training and promotion, and working conditions (OJ L 39, 14.2.1976, p. 40).
— Council Directive 79/7/EEC of 19 December 1978 on the progressive implementation of the principle of equal treatment for men and women in matters of social security (OJ L 6, 10.1.1979, p. 24).
— Council Directive 86/378/EEC of 24 July 1986 on the implementation of the principle of equal treatment for men and women in occupational social security schemes (OJ L 225, 12.8.1986, p. 40).
— Council Directive 86/613/EEC of 11 December 1986 on the application of the principle of equal treatment between men and women engaged in an activity, including agriculture, in a self-employed capacity, and on the protection of self-employed women during pregnancy and motherhood (OJ L 359, 19.12.1986, p. 56).
— Council Directive 92/85/EEC of 19 October 1992 on the introduction of measures to encourage improvements in the safety and health at work of pregnant workers and workers who have recently given birth or are breastfeeding (OJ L 348, 28.11.1992, p. 1).

[4] — Council Decision 95/593/EC of 22 December 1995 on a medium-term Community action programme on equal opportunities for men and women (1996-2000) (OJ L 335, 30.12.1995, p. 37).

[5] — Council Recommendation 84/635/EEC of 13 December 1984 on the promotion of positive action for women (OJ L 331, 19.12.1984, p. 34).
— Council Recommendation 92/241/EEC of 31 March 1992 on child care (OJ L 123, 8.5.1992, p. 16).

[6] — Council resolution of 12 July 1982 on the promotion of equal opportunities for women (OJ C 186, 21.7.1982, p. 3).
— Council resolution of 7 June 1984 on action to combat unemployment amongst women (OJ C 161, 21.6.1984, p. 4).
— Resolution of the Council and the Ministers for Education, meeting within the Council, of 3 June 1985 containing an action programme on equal opportunities for girls and boys in education (OJ C 166, 5.7.1985, p. 1).
— Second Council resolution of 24 July 1986 on the promotion of equal opportunities for women (OJ C 203, 12.8.1986, p. 2).
— Council resolution of 16 December 1988 on the reintegration and late integration of women into working life (OJ C 333, 28.12.1988, p. 1).
— Council resolution of 29 May 1990 on the protection of the dignity of women and men at work (OJ C 157, 27.6.1990, p. 3).
— Council resolution of 21 May 1991 on the third medium-term Community action programme on equal opportunities for women and men (1991-95) (OJ C 142, 31.5.1991, p. 1).
— Council resolution of 22 June 1994 on the promotion of equal opportunities for women and men through action by the European Structural Funds (OJ C 231, 20.8.1994, p. 1).
— Resolution of the Council and of the Representatives of the Governments of the Member States, meeting within the Council, of 6 December 1994 on equal participation by women in an employment-intensive economic growth strategy within the European Union (OJ C 368, 23.12.1994, p. 3).
— Council resolution of 27 March 1995 on the balanced participation of women and men in decision-making (OJ C 168, 4.7.1995, p. 3).
— Resolution of the Council and of the Representatives of the Governments of the Member States, meeting within the Council, of 5 October 1995 on the image of women and men portrayed in advertising and the media (OJ C 296, 10.11.1995, p. 15).

(2) Whereas the Heads of State or Government, meeting within the European Council in Essen, Cannes and Madrid, stressed that the fight against unemployment and equal opportunities for women and men were paramount tasks of the European Union and its Member States;

(3) Whereas attention was focused on women's access to decision-making in Council Recommendation 84/635/EEC of 13 December 1984 on the promotion of positive action for women [1], in the second Council Resolution of 24 July 1986 on the promotion of equal opportunities for women [2], in the Council Resolution of 21 May 1991 on the third medium-term Community action programme on equal opportunities for women and men (1991-95) [3], in the Council Resolution of 27 March 1995 on the balanced participation of women and men in decision-making [4] and in Council Decision 95/593/EC of 22 December 1995 on a medium-term Community action programme on equal opportunities for men and women (1996-2000) [5];

(4) Whereas the European Parliament in its Resolution of 11 February 1994 on women in decision-making bodies [6] asked the Commission to 'step up implementation of the equal opportunities policy set out in the third Community action programme, to combat individual obstacles which hinder women from taking part in decision-making' and to define 'measures and actions to promote greater participation of women in the decision-making process';

(5) Whereas the Declaration and the Platform for Action of the Fourth World Conference on Women (Beijing, 4 to 15 September 1995) stressed the need to ensure that responsibilities, powers and rights are shared equally; whereas the Member States are committed to implementing the Platform for Action;

(6) Whereas participation in the decision-making process depends on representation on decision-making bodies at all levels of political, economic, social and cultural life and requires, in particular, presence in posts of responsibility and decision-taking positions;

(7) Whereas women are still under-represented in decision-making bodies, in the political, economic, social and cultural spheres;

(8) Whereas the under-representation of women in decision-making bodies is partly a result of the delay in women attaining equal civic and civil rights, of obstacles to their gaining economic independence and of difficulties in reconciling their working and family life;

(9) Whereas balanced participation of women and men in the decision-making process is a requirement for democracy;

(10) Whereas the under-representation of women in decision-making posts constitutes a loss for society as a whole and may prevent the interests and needs of the entire population from being catered for in full;

(11) Whereas measures aimed at bringing about a balanced participation of women and men in the decision-making process in all sectors should go together with the integration of the dimension of equality of opportunity for women and men in all policies and actions;

(12) Whereas balanced participation of women and men in the decision-making process is likely to give rise to different ideas, values and behaviour which will result in more justice and equality in the world for both men and women;

(13) Whereas the Member States, the social partners, political parties and organisations, non-governmental organisations and the media play a key role in creating a society where

---

[1] OJ L 331, 19.12.1984, p. 34.
[2] OJ C 203, 12.8.1986, p. 2.
[3] OJ C 142, 31.5.1991, p. 1.
[4] OJ C 168, 4.7.1995, p. 3.
[5] OJ L 335, 30.12.1995, p. 37.
[6] OJ C 61, 28.2.1994, p. 248.

there is a gender balance in the exercise of responsibilities in the political, economic, social and cultural spheres;

(14) Whereas it is appropriate to adopt guidelines to promote balanced participation of women and men in the decision-making process with the aim of bringing about equality of opportunity for women and men and whereas it is appropriate, within the framework of the medium-term Community action programme on equal opportunities for men and women (1996-2000), to make those guidelines more effective through the exchange of information on good practice;

(15) Whereas the provisions of this Recommendation apply solely within the limits of Community competence; whereas equal treatment for male and female workers constitutes one of the objectives of the Community, insofar as the harmonisation of living and working conditions while maintaining their improvement are, *inter alia,* to be furthered;

(16) Whereas the Treaty does not confer, for the adoption of this Recommendation, any other powers than those referred to in Article 235,

I. RECOMMENDS THAT THE MEMBER STATES:

1. adopt a comprehensive, integrated strategy designed to promote balanced participation of women and men in the decision-making process and develop or introduce the appropriate measures to achieve this, such as, where necessary, legislative and/or regulatory measures and/or incentives;

2. (a) alert those involved in education and training at all levels, including those responsible for teaching materials, to the importance of:

   — a realistic and complete image of the roles and abilities of women and men in society, free of prejudice and discriminatory stereotypes,

   — a more balanced sharing of professional, domestic and social responsibilities between women and men, and

   — balanced participation of women and men in the decision-making process at all levels;

   (b) at all levels of education and training, encourage girls and women to take part and express themselves in education and training activities as actively and fully as boys and men, so as to prepare them for an active role in society, including political, economic, social and cultural life, and in particular in decision-making processes;

   (c) make public opinion aware of the importance of disseminating an image of women and men that neither reinforces nor consolidates discriminatory stereotyping of women's and men's responsibilities;

   (d) without encroaching on their autonomy, encourage and support efforts of associations and organisations in all areas of society to promote women's access to the decision-making process and balanced participation by women and men in decision-making bodies;

   (e) without prejudice to their autonomy, encourage and support the efforts of the social partners to promote balanced participation of women and men in their activities and highlight the social partners' responsibility for promoting and proposing women candidates for nomination to various assignments on public commissions and committees in the Member States and at Community level;

   (f) devise, launch and promote public campaigns to alert public opinion to the usefulness and advantages for society as a whole of balanced participation by women and men in decision-making;

3. (a) promote or improve the collection and publication of statistics to provide a clearer picture of how women and men are represented at all levels of the decision-making process in the political, economic, social and cultural spheres;

   (b) support, develop and encourage quantitative and qualitative studies on the participation of women and men in the decision-making process, and especially:

   — on the legal, social or cultural obstacles impeding access to and participation in the decision-making process for persons of either sex,

   — on strategies for overcoming such obstacles, and

   — on the utility and advantages for society and for the operation of democracy of a better balance between the sexes in the decision-making process;

   (c) promote, support and encourage initiatives creating examples of good practice in the various areas of the decision-making process and develop programmes for the dissemination and exchange of experience with a view to propagating activities;

4. (a) promote balanced participation by women and men at all levels in governmental bodies and committees;

   (b) raise the awareness of those involved of the importance of taking initiatives to achieve balanced participation of women and men in public positions at all levels, paying particular attention to the promotion of a balanced composition in committees, commissions and working parties at national as well as Community level;

   (c) provide for, implement or develop a coherent set of measures encouraging equal opportunities in the public sector and respecting the concept of balanced participation in the decision-making process, and ensure, when recruitment competitions take place, that women and men are, as far as possible, represented equally in the committees responsible for preparing competitions and in the selection boards;

   (d) encourage the private sector to increase the presence of women at all levels of decision-making, notably by the adoption of, or within the framework of, equality plans and positive action programmes;

II. CALLS ON THE INSTITUTIONS, SUBSIDIARY BODIES AND DECENTRALISED BODIES OF THE EUROPEAN COMMUNITIES TO:

design a strategy for achieving balanced participation by women and men in the decision-making process in each institution, subsidiary body and decentralised body of the European Communities;

III. CALLS ON THE COMMISSION TO:

1. encourage and organise, within the framework of Council Decision 95/593/EC of 22 December 1995 on a medium-term Community action programme on equal opportunities for men and women (1996-2000), systematic pooling of information and experience between Member States on good practice and the assessment of the impact of measures taken to achieve a better balance between women and men in the decision-making process;

2. to this end, and within that framework, step up its efforts to provide information, alert public opinion, encourage research and promote schemes aimed at achieving balanced participation by women and men in the decision-making process;

3. submit a report to the European Parliament, the Council and the Economic and Social Committee, for the first time three years after adoption of this Recommendation and thereafter annually, on its implementation, on the basis of the information provided by the Member States and the institutions, subsidiary bodies and decentralised bodies of the European Communities.

Done at Brussels, 2 December 1996.

For the Council
The President
E. FITZGERALD

COUNCIL RECOMMENDATION (92/241/EEC)

of 31 March 1992

on child care

THE COUNCIL OF THE EUROPEAN COMMUNITIES,

Having regard to the Treaty establishing the European Economic Community, and in particular Article 235 thereof,

Having regard to the proposal from the Commission [1],

Having regard to the opinion of the European Parliament [2],

Having regard to the opinion of the Economic and Social Committee [3],

Whereas the Community Charter of the Fundamental Social Rights of Workers, adopted in the Strasbourg European Council on 9 December 1989 by the Heads of State or Government of eleven Member States, lays down, in the third paragraph of point 16 in particular, that:

'Measures should also be developed to enable men and women to reconcile their occupational and family obligations';

Whereas the Commission action programme implementing the Community Charter provides for this Recommendation;

Whereas in its third medium-term action programme on equal opportunities for women and men (1991-95), the Commission identified the need for further action in this area;

Whereas in its communication on family policies, sent to the Council on 24 August 1989, the Commission emphasised the importance of intensifying work relating to child care;

Whereas child-care methods, parental leave and maternity leave form part of a whole which enables people to combine their family responsibilities and occupational ambitions;

Whereas the Member States should take and/or encourage initiatives, taking into account the responsibilities of national, regional and local authorities, management and labour, other relevant organisations and private individuals, and/or in cooperation with the various parties concerned;

Whereas the reconciliation of occupational, family and upbringing responsabilities arising from the care of children has to be viewed in a wide perspective which also takes into account the particular interests and needs of children at different age levels, where it is important, in order to achieve this, to encourage an overall policy aimed at enabling such reconciliation to occur;

Whereas it is essential to promote the well-being of children and families, ensuring that their various needs are met and taking into account the fact that responsabilities arising from the care and upbringing of children continue up to and throughout the period of children's schooling, and especially when they are younger;

Whereas in all Member States the demand for child-care services at prices affordable to parents exceeds the existing supply;

Whereas inadequate provision of child-care services at prices affordable to parents and other initiatives to reconcile responsibility for the family and the upbringing of children with the employment, or with the education and training of parents in order to obtain employment constitutes a major barrier to women's access to and more effective participation in the labour market, on equal terms with men, the effective participation of women in all areas of society and the effective use of their talents, skills and abilities in the current demographic situation;

Whereas, moreover, in this area, disparities exist between Member States and between regions within Member States;

Whereas, furthermore, better child-care services could facilitate freedom of movement of workers and mobility on the European labour market;

Whereas child-care services may be public or private, individual or collective in form;

Whereas child care is a broad concept which may involve the provision of child-care services which answer the needs of children, the grant of special leave to parents and the development of a working environment structure and organisation which is adapted to the sharing between women and men of occupational, family and upbringing responsibilities arising from the care of children;

[1] OJ C 242, 17.9.1991, p. 3.
[2] OJ C 326, 16.12.1991, p. 279.
[3] OJ C 40, 17.2.1992, p. 88.

Whereas in certain Member States, owing to the low level of national income and the need to impose strict limits on growth in public expenditure, the role of the public authorities may be subject to particular constraints;

Whereas the standard clause included in the Community support frameworks for structural policy stipulates that the actions and measures taken within such a framework must conform with and, where appropriate, contribute to the implementation of Community policy and legislation relating to equality of opportunity between women and men, and that in particular, consideration must be given to training and infrastructure requirements which facilitate labour force participation by women with children;

Whereas, furthermore, in the NOW Community initiative (1991-93), financed by the Structural Funds, for the promotion of equal opportunities for women in the fields of employment and vocational training, additional child-care measures are provided for to assist women with children to have access to the labour market and to vocational training courses,

HEREBY RECOMMENDS AS FOLLOWS:

Article 1

Objective

It is recommended that Member States should take and/or progressively encourage initiatives to enable women and men to reconcile their occupational, family and upbringing responsibilities arising from the care of children.

Article 2

Areas of initiatives

For the purposes of Article 1, it is recommended that the Member States, taking into account the respective responsibilities of national, regional and local authorities, management and labour, other relevant organisations and private individuals, and/or in cooperation with national, regional or local authorities, management and labour, other relevant organisations and private individuals, should take and/or encourage initiatives in the following four areas:

1. The provision of children-care services while parents:

   — are working,

   — are following a course of education or training in order to obtain employment

      or

   — are seeking a job or a course of education or training in order to obtain employment.

   For the purposes of this Recommendation, 'child-care services' means any type of child care, whether public or private, individual or collective.

2. Special leave for employed parents with responsibility for the care and upbringing of children.

3. The environment, structure and organisation of work, to make them responsive to the needs of workers with children.

4. The sharing of occupational, family and upbringing responsibilities arising from the care of children between women and men.

Article 3

Child-care services

As regards child-care services, it is recommended that the Member States, taking into account the respective responsabilities of national, regional and local authorities, management and labour, other relevant organisations and private individuals, and/or in cooperation with national, regional or local authorities, management and labour, other relevant organisations and private individuals, should take and/or encourage initiatives to:

1. enable parents who are working, following a course of education or training in order to obtain employment or are seeking employment or a course of education or training in order to obtain employment to have as much access as possible to local child-care services.

   In this context, endeavours should in particular be made to ensure that:

   — the services are offered at prices affordable to parents;

   — they combine reliable care from the point of view of health and safety with a general upbringing and a pedagogical approach;

   — the needs of parents and children are taken into account when access to services is determined;

   — the services are available in all areas and regions of Member States, both in urban areas and in rural areas;

   — the services are accessible to children with special needs, for example linguistic needs, and to children in single-parent families, and meet the needs of such children;

2. encourage flexibility and diversity of child-care services as part of a strategy to increase choice and

meet the different preferences, needs and circumstances of children and their parents, while preserving coherence between different services;

3. endeavour that the training, both initial and continuous, of workers in child-care services is appropriate to the importance and the social and educative value of their work;

4. encourage child-care services to work closely with local communities through regular contact and exchanges of information, so as to be responsive to parental needs and particular local circumstances;

5. encourage national, regional or local authorities, management and labour, other relevant organisations and private individuals, in accordance with their respective responsibilities, to make a financial contribution to the creation and/or operation of coherent child-care services which can be afforded by parents and which offer them a choice.

Article 4

Special leave

As regards special leave for employed parents with responsibility for the care and upbringing of children, it is recommended that Member States, taking into account the respective responsibilities of national, regional and local authorities, management and labour, other relevant organisations and private individuals, and/or in cooperation with national, regional or local authorities, management and labour, other relevant organisations and private individuals, should take and/or encourage initiatives, to take realistic account of women's increased participation in the labour force.

These initiatives should concern, for example, special leave enabling employed parents, both men and women, who so desire properly to discharge their occupational, family and upbringing responsibilities, with, *inter alia,* some flexibility as to how leave may be taken.

Article 5

Environment, structure and organisation of work

As regards the environment, structure and organisation of work, it is recommended that Member States, taking

into account the respective responsibilities of national, regional and local authorities, management and labour, other relevant organisations and private individuals, and/or in cooperation with national, regional or local authorities, management and labour, other relevant authorities and private individuals, should take and/or encourage initiatives to:

1. support action, in particular within the framework of collective agreements, to create an environment, structure and organisation of work which take into account the needs of all working parents with responsibility for the care and upbringing of children;

2. ensure that due recognition is given to persons engaged in child-care services as regards the way in which they work and the social value of their work;

3. promote action, especially in the public sector, which can serve as an example in developing initiatives in this area.

Article 6

Sharing of responsibilities

As regards responsibilities arising from the care and upbringing of children, it is recommended that Member States should promote and encourage, with due respect for freedom of the individual, increased participation by men, in order to a achieve a more equal sharing of parental responsibilities between men and women and to enable women to have a more effective role in the labour market.

Article 7

Commission report

The Member States shall inform the Commission, within three years of the date of the adoption of this Recommendation, of the measures taken to give effect to it, in order to enable the Commission to draw up a report on its implementation.

Done at Brussels, 31 March 1992.

For the Council
The President
Vitor MARTINS

COUNCIL RECOMMENDATION (84/635/EEC)

of 13 December 1984

on the promotion of positive action for women

THE COUNCIL OF THE EUROPEAN COMMUNITIES,

Having regard to the Treaty establishing the European Economic Community, and in particular Article 235 thereof,

Having regard to the draft recommendation submitted by the Commission [1],

Having regard to the opinion of the European Parliament [2],

Having regard to the opinion of the Economic and Social Committee [3],

Whereas various action has been undertaken at Community level to promote equal opportunities for women; whereas, in particular the Council adopted, on the basis of Articles 100 and 235 of the Treaty, Directives 75/117/EEC [4], 76/207/EEC [5] and 79/7/EEC [6] concerning equal treatment for men and women; whereas other legal instruments are being prepared;

Whereas Article 2 (4) of Council Directive 76/207/EEC provides that it shall be without prejudice to measures to promote equal opportunities for men and women, in particular by removing existing inequalities which affect women's opportunities in the areas referred to in Article 1 (1) thereof;

Whereas existing legal provisions on equal treatment, which are designed to afford rights to individuals, are inadequate for the elimination of all existing inequalities unless parallel action is taken by governments, both sides of industry and other bodies concerned, to counteract the prejudicial effects on women in employment which arise from social attitudes, behaviour and structures;

Whereas, by its resolution of 12 July 1982 on the promotion of equal opportunities for women [7], the Council approved the general objectives of the new Community action programme on the promotion of equal opportunities for women (1982 to 1985), namely the stepping up of action to ensure observance of the principle of equal treatment and the promotion of equal op-

portunities in practice by positive action (Part B of the programme), and expressed the will to implement appropriate measures to achieve these objectives;

Whereas, in a period of economic crisis, action taken should be not only continued but also intensified at national level and Community level with a view to promoting the achievement of equal opportunities in practice through the implementation of positive actions, more especially in the fields of equal pay and equal treatment as regards access to employment, vocational training and promotion and working conditions;

Whereas the European Parliament has underlined the importance of positive action,

HEREBY RECOMMENDS MEMBER STATES:

1. To adopt a positive action policy designed to eliminate existing inequalities affecting women in working life and to promote a better balance between the sexes in employment, comprising appropriate general and specific measures, within the framework of national policies and practices, while fully respecting the spheres of competence of the two sides of industry, in order:

   (a) to eliminate or counteract the prejudicial effects on women in employment or seeking employment which arise from existing attitudes, behaviour and structures based on the idea of a traditional division of roles in society between men and women;

   (b) to encourage the participation of women in various occupations in those sectors of working life where they are at present under-represented, particularly in the sectors of the future, and at higher levels of responsibility in order to achieve better use of all human resources.

2. To establish a framework containing appropriate provisions designed to promote and facilitate the introduction and extension of such measures.

3. To take, continue or promote positive action measures in the public and private sectors.

4. To take steps to ensure that positive action includes as far as possible actions having a bearing on the following aspects:

   — informing and increasing the awareness of both the general public and the working world of the need to promote equality of opportunity for working women,

---

[1] OJ C 143, 30.5.1984, p. 3.
[2] OJ C 315, 26.11.1984, p. 81.
[3] Opinion delivered on 12 November 1984 (not yet published in the Official Journal).
[4] OJ L 45, 19.2.1975, p. 19.
[5] OJ L 39, 14.2.1976, p. 40.
[6] OJ L 6, 10.1.1979, p. 24.
[7] OJ C 186, 21.7.1982, p. 3.

— respect for the dignity of women at the work-place,

— qualitative and quantitative studies and analyses of the position of women on the labour market,

— diversification of vocational choice, and more relevant vocational skills, particularly through appropriate vocational training, including the implementation of supporting measures and suitable teaching methods,

— measures necessary to ensure that placement, guidance and counselling services have sufficient skilled personnel to provide a service based on the necessary expertise in the special problems of unemployed women,

— encouraging women candidates and the recruitment and promotion of women in sectors and professions and at levels where they are under-represented, particularly as regards positions of responsibility,

— adapting working conditions; adjusting the organisation of work and working time,

— encouraging supporting measures such as those designed to foster greater sharing of occupational and social responsibilities,

— active participation by women in decision-making bodies, including those representing workers, employers and the self-employed.

5. To ensure that the actions and measures described in points 1 to 4 are made known to the public and to the working world, especially to potential beneficiaries, by all appropriate means and as extensively as possible.

6. To enable national equal opportunities committees and organisations to make a significant contribution to the promotion of such measures, which pre-supposes that these committees and organisations are provided with appropriate means of action.

7. To encourage both sides of industry, wherever possible, to promote positive action within their own organisations and the work place, for example by suggesting guidelines, principles, codes of good conduct or good practice or any other appropriate formula for the implementation of such action.

8. To make efforts also in the public sector to promote equal opportunities which might serve as an example, particularly in those fields where new information technologies are being used or developed.

9. To make appropriate arrangements to gather information on measures taken by public and private bodies, and to follow up and evaluate such measures,

AND TO THIS END REQUESTS THE COMMISSION:

1. To promote and organise in liaison with the Member States the systematic exchange and assessment of information and experience on positive action within the Community.

2. To submit a report to the Council, within three years of the adoption of this recommendation, on progress achieved in its implementation, on the basis of information supplied to it by Member States.

Done at Brussels, 13 December 1984.

For the Council
The President
R. QUINN

Commission recommendations

COMMISSION RECOMMENDATION (92/131/EEC)

of 27 November 1991

on the protection of the dignity of women and men at work

THE COMMISSION OF THE EUROPEAN COMMUNITIES,

Having regard to the Treaty establishing the European Economic Community, and in particular the second indent of Article 155 thereof,

Whereas unwanted conduct of a sexual nature, or other conduct based on sex affecting the dignity of women and men at work, including the conduct of superiors and colleagues, is unacceptable and may, in certain circumstances, be contrary to the principle of equal treatment within the meaning of Articles 3, 4 and 5 of Council Directive 76/207/EEC of 9 February 1976 on the implementation of the principle of equal treatment for men and women as regards access to employment, vocational training and promotion, and working conditions [1], a view supported by case-law in some Member States;

Whereas, in accordance with the Council recommendation of 13 December 1984 on the promotion of positive action for women [2], many Member States have carried out a variety of positive action measures and actions having a bearing, *inter alia,* on respect for the dignity of women at the workplace;

Whereas the European Parliament, in its resolution of 11 June 1986 on violence against women [3], has called upon national governments, equal opportunities committees and trade unions to carry out concerted information campaigns to create a proper awareness of the individual rights of all members of the labour force;

Whereas the Advisory Committee on Equal Opportunities for Women and Men, in its opinion of 20 June 1988, has unanimously recommended that there should be a recommendation and code of conduct on sexual harassment in the workplace covering harassment of both sexes;

Whereas the Commission in its action programme relating to the implementation of the Community Charter of Basic Social Rights for Workers undertook to examine the protection of workers and their dignity at work, having regard to the reports and recommendations prepared on various aspects of implementation of Community law [4];

Whereas the Council, in its resolution of 29 May 1990 on the protection of the dignity of women and men at work [5], affirms that conduct based on sex affecting the dignity of women and men at work, including conduct of superiors and colleagues, constitutes an intolerable violation of the dignity of workers or trainees, and calls on the Member States and the institutions and organs of the European Communities to develop positive measures designed to create a climate at work in which women and men respect one another's human integrity;

Whereas the Commission, in its third action programme on equal opportunities for women and men, 1991 to 1995, and pursuant to paragraph 3 (2) of the said Council resolution of 29 May 1990, resolved to draw up a code of conduct on the protection of the dignity of women and men at work [6], based on experience and best practice in the Member States, to provide guidance on initiating and pursuing positive measures designed to create a climate at work in which women and men respect one another's human integrity;

Whereas the European Parliament, on 22 October 1991, adopted a resolution on the protection of the dignity of women and men at work [7];

Whereas the Economic and Social Committee, on 30 October 1991, adopted an opinion on the protection of the dignity of women and men at work [8],

RECOMMENDS AS FOLLOWS:

Article 1

It is recommended that the Member States take action to promote awareness that conduct of a sexual nature, or other conduct based on sex affecting the dignity of women and men at work, including conduct of superiors and colleagues, is unacceptable if:

(a) such conduct is unwanted, unreasonable and offensive to the recipient;

(b) a person's rejection of, or submission to, such conduct on the part of employers or workers (including superiors or colleagues) is used explicitly or implicitly as a basis for a decision which affects that person's access to vocational training, access

---

[1] OJ L 39, 14.2.1976, p. 40.

[2] OJ L 331, 19.12.1984, p. 34.

[3] OJ C 176, 14.7.1986, p. 79.

[4] COM(89) 568 final, 29.11.1989. For example, 'The dignity of women at work: a report on the problem of sexual harassment in the Member States of the European Communities', October 1987, by Michael Rubenstein (ISBN 92-825-8764-9).

[5] OJ C 157, 27.6.1990, p. 3.

[6] COM(90) 449 final, 6.11.1990.

[7] OJ C 305, 25.11.1991.

[8] OJ C 14, 20.1.1992.

to employment, continued employment, promotion, salary or any other employment decisions;

and/or

(c) such conduct creates an intimidating, hostile or humiliating work environment for the recipient;

and that such conduct may, in certain circumstances, be contrary to the principle of equal treatment within the meaning of Articles 3, 4 and 5 of Directive 76/207/EEC.

Article 2

It is recommended that Member States take action, in the public sector, to implement the Commission's code of practice on the protection of the dignity of women and men at work, annexed hereto. The action of the Member States, in thus initiating and pursuing positive measures designed to create a climate at work in which women and men respect one another's human integrity, should serve as an example to the private sector.

Article 3

It is recommended that Member States encourage employers and employee representatives to develop measures to implement the Commission's code of practice on the protection of the dignity of women and men at work.

Article 4

Member States shall inform the Commission within three years of the date of this recommendation of the measures taken to give effect to it, in order to allow the Commission to draw up a report on all such measures. The Commission shall, within this period, ensure the widest possible circulation of the code of practice. The report should examine the degree of awareness of the Code, its perceived effectiveness, its degree of application and the extent of its use in collective bargaining between the social partners.

Article 5

This recommendation is addressed to the Member States.

Done at Brussels, 27 November 1991.

For the Commission
Vasso PAPANDREOU
Member of the Commission

ANNEX

PROTECTING THE DIGNITY OF WOMEN AND MEN AT WORK

A code of practice on measures to combat sexual harassment

1. INTRODUCTION

This code of practice is issued in accordance with the resolution of the Council of Ministers on the protection of the dignity of women and men at work ([1]), and to accompany the Commission's recommendation on this issue.

Its purpose is to give practical guidance to employers, trade unions, and employees on the protection of the dignity of women and men at work. The code is intended to be applicable in both the public and the private sector and employers are encouraged to follow the recommendations contained in the code in a way which is appropriate to the size and structure of their organisation. It may be particularly relevant for small and medium-sized enterprises to adapt some of the practical steps to their specific needs.

The aim is to ensure that sexual harassment does not occur and, if it does occur, to ensure that adequate procedures are readily available to deal with the problem and prevent its recurrence. The code thus seeks to encourage the development and implementation of policies and practices which establish working environments free of sexual harassment and in which women and men respect one another's human integrity.

The expert report carried out on behalf of the Commission found that sexual harassment is a serious problem for many working women in the European Community ([2]) and research in Member States has proven beyond doubt that sexual harassment at work is not an isolated phenomenon. On the contrary, it is clear that for millions of women in the European Community, sexual harassment is an unpleasant and unavoidable part of their working lives. Men too may suffer sexual harassment and should, of course, have the same rights as women to the protection of their dignity.

Some specific groups are particularly vulnerable to sexual harassment. Research in several Member States, which documents the link between the risk of sexual harassment and the recipient's perceived vulnerability, suggests that divorced and separated women, young women and new entrants to the labour market and those with irregular or precarious employment contracts, women in non-traditional jobs, women with disabilities, lesbians and women from racial

minorities are disproportionately at risk. Gay men and young men are also vulnerable to harassment. It is undeniable that harassment on grounds of sexual orientation undermines the dignity at work of those affected and it is impossible to regard such harassment as appropriate workplace behaviour.

Sexual harassment pollutes the working environment and can have a devastating effect upon the health, confidence, morale and performance of those affected by it. The anxiety and stress produced by sexual harassment commonly leads to those subjected to it taking time off work due to sickness, being less efficient at work, or leaving their job to seek work elsewhere. Employees often suffer the adverse consequences of the harassment itself and short- and long-term damage to their employment prospects if they are forced to change jobs. Sexual harassment may also have a damaging impact on employees not themselves the object of unwanted behaviour but who are witness to it or have a knowledge of the unwanted behaviour.

There are also adverse consequences arising from sexual harassment for employers. It has a direct impact on the profitability of the enterprise where staff take sick leave or resign their posts because of sexual harassment, and on the economic efficiency of the enterprise where employees' productivity is reduced by having to work in a climate in which individuals' integrity is not respected.

In general terms, sexual harassment is an obstacle to the proper integration of women into the labour market and the Commission is committed to encouraging the development of comprehensive measures to improve such integration ([3]).

2. DEFINITION

Sexual harassment means unwanted conduct of a sexual nature, or other conduct based on sex affecting the dignity of women and men at work ([3]). This can include unwelcome physical, verbal or non-verbal conduct.

Thus, a range of behaviour may be considered to constitute sexual harassment. It is unacceptable if such conduct is unwanted, unreasonable and offensive to the recipient; a person's rejection of or submission to such conduct on the part of employers or workers (including superiors or colleagues) is used explicitly or implicitly as a basis for a decision which affects that

---

[1] OJ C 157, 27.6.1990, p. 3.
[2] 'The dignity of women at work: a report on the problem of sexual harassment in the Member States of the European Communities', October 1987, by Michael Rubenstein (ISBN 92-825-8764-9).

[3] Third action programme on equal opportunities for women and men, 1991 to 1995, COM(90) 449, 6.11.1990.

person's access to vocational training or to employment, continued employment, promotion, salary or any other employment decisions; and/or such conduct creates an intimidating, hostile or humiliating working environment for the recipient [1].

The essential characteristic of sexual harassment is that it is unwanted by the recipient, that it is for each individual to determine what behaviour is acceptable to them and what they regard as offensive. Sexual attention becomes sexual harassment if it is persisted in once it has been made clear that it is regarded by the recipient as offensive, although one incident of harassment may constitute sexual harassment if sufficiently serious. It is the unwanted nature of the conduct which distinguishes sexual harassment from friendly behaviour, which is welcome and mutual.

3. THE LAW AND EMPLOYERS' RESPONSIBILITIES

Conduct of a sexual nature or other based on sex affecting the dignity of women and men at work may be contrary to the principle of equal treatment within the meaning of Articles 3, 4 and 5 of Council Directive 76/207/EEC of 9 February 1976 on the implementation of the principle of equal treatment for men and women as regards access to employment, vocational training and promotion, and working conditions [2]. This principle means that there shall be no discrimination whatsoever on grounds of sex either directly or indirectly by reference in particular to marital or family status.

In certain circumstances, and depending upon national law, sexual harassment may also be a criminal offence or may contravene other obligations imposed by the law, such as health and safety duties, or a duty, contractual or otherwise, to be a good employer. Since sexual harassment is a form of employee misconduct, employers have a responsibility to deal with it as they do with any other form of employee misconduct as well as to refrain from harassing employees themselves. Since sexual harassment is a risk to health and safety, employers have a responsibility to take steps to minimise the risk as they do with other hazards. Since sexual harassment often entails an abuse of power, employers may have a responsibility for the misuse of the authority they delegate.

This code, however, focuses on sexual harassment as a problem of sex discrimination. Sexual harassment is sex discrimination because the gender of the recipient is the determining factor in who is harassed. Conduct of a sexual nature or other conduct based on sex affecting the dignity of women and men at work in some Member States already has been found to contravene national equal treatment laws and employers have a re-

sponsibility to seek to ensure that the work environment is free from such conduct [3].

As sexual harassment is often a function of women's status in the employment hierarchy, policies to deal with sexual harassment are likely to be most effective where they are linked to a broader policy to promote equal opportunities and to improve the position of women. Advice on steps which can be taken generally to implement an equal opportunities policy is set out in the Commission's guide to positive action [4].

Similarly, a procedure to deal with complaints of sexual harassment should be regarded as only one component of a strategy to deal with the problem. The prime objective should be to change behaviour and attitudes, to seek to ensure the prevention of sexual harassment.

4. COLLECTIVE BARGAINING

The majority of the recommendations contained in this code are for action by employers, since employers have clear responsibilities to ensure the protection of the dignity of women and men at work.

Trade unions also have responsibilities to their members and they can and should play an important role in the prevention of sexual harassment in the workplace. It is recommended that the question of including appropriate clauses in agreements be examined in the context of the collective bargaining process, with the aim of achieving a work environment free from unwanted conduct of a sexual nature or other conduct based on sex affecting the dignity of women and men at work and free from victimisation of a complainant or of a person wishing to give, or giving, evidence in the event of a complaint.

5. RECOMMENDATIONS TO EMPLOYERS

The policies and procedures recommended below should be adopted, where appropriate, after consultation or negotiation with trade unions or employee representatives. Experience suggests that strategies to create and maintain a working environment in which the dignity of employees is respected are most likely to be effective where they are jointly agreed.

It should be emphasised that a distinguishing characteristic of sexual harassment is that employees subjected to it often will be reluctant to complain. An absence of complaints about sexual harassment in a particular organisation, therefore, does not necessarily

---

[1] Council resolution on the protection of the dignity of women and men at work (OJ C 157, 27.6.1990, p. 3, point 1).

[2] OJ L 39, 14.2.1976, p. 40.

[3] Council resolution on the protection of the dignity of women and men at work (OJ C 157, 27.6.1990, p. 3, point 2 (3) (a)).

[4] *Positive action: Equal opportunities for women in employment — a guide,* Office for Official Publications of the European Communities, 1988.

mean an absence of sexual harassment. It may mean that the recipients of sexual harassment think that there is no point in complaining because nothing will be done about it, or because it will be trivialised or the complainant subjected to ridicule, or because they fear reprisals. Implementing the preventative and procedural recommendations outlined below should facilitate the creation of a climate at work in which such concerns have no place.

A. **Prevention**

(i) *Policy statements*

As a first step in showing senior management's concern and their commitment to dealing with the problem of sexual harassment, employers should issue a policy statement which expressly states that all employees have a right to be treated with dignity, that sexual harassment at work will not be permitted or condoned and that employees have a right to complain about it should it occur.

It is recommended that the policy statement make clear what is considered inappropriate behaviour at work, and explain that such behaviour, in certain circumstances, may be unlawful. It is advisable for the statement to set out a positive duty on managers and supervisors to implement the policy and to take corrective action to ensure compliance with it. It should also place a positive duty on all employees to comply with the policy and to ensure that their colleagues are treated with respect and dignity.

In addition, it is recommended that the statement explain the procedure which should be followed by employees subjected to sexual harassment at work in order to obtain assistance and to whom they should complain; that it contain an undertaking that allegations of sexual harassment will be dealt with seriously, expeditiously and confidentially, and that employees will be protected against victimisation or retaliation for bringing a complaint of sexual harassment. It should also specify that appropriate disciplinary measures will be taken against employees found guilty of sexual harassment.

(ii) *Communicating the policy*

Once the policy has been developed, it is important to ensure that it is communicated effectively to all employees, so that they are aware that they have a right to complain and to whom they should complain; that their complaint will be dealt with promptly and fairly; and that employees are made aware of the likely consequences of engaging in sexual harassment. Such communication will highlight management's commitment to eliminating sexual harassment, thus enhancing a climate in which it will not occur.

(iii) *Responsibility*

All employees have a responsibility to help to ensure a working environment in which the dignity of employees is respected and managers (including supervisors) have a particular duty to ensure that sexual harassment does not occur in work areas for which they are responsible. It is recommended that managers explain the organisation's policy to their staff and take steps to positively promote the policy. Managers should also be responsive and supportive to any member of staff who complains about sexual harassment, provide full and clear advice on the procedure to be adopted, maintain confidentiality in any cases of sexual harassment and ensure that there is no further problem of sexual harassment or any victimisation after a complaint has been resolved.

(iv) *Training*

An important means of ensuring that sexual harassment does not occur and that, if it does occur, the problem is resolved efficiently is through the provision of training for managers and supervisors. Such training should aim to identify the factors which contribute to a working environment free of sexual harassment and to familiarise participants with their responsibilities under the employer's policy and any problems they are likely to encounter.

In addition, those playing an official role in any formal complaints procedure in respect of sexual harassment should receive specialist training, such as that outlined above.

It is also good practice to include information as to the organisation's policy on sexual harassment and procedures for dealing with it as part of appropriate induction and training programmes.

B. **Procedures**

The development of clear and precise procedures to deal with sexual harassment once it has occurred is of great importance. The procedures should ensure the resolution of problems in an efficient and effective manner. Practical guidance for employees on how to deal with sexual harassment when it occurs and with its aftermath will make it more likely that it will be dealt with at an early stage. Such guidance should of course draw attention to an employee's legal rights and to any time limits within which they must be exercised.

(i) *Resolving problems informally*

Most recipients of harassment simply want the harassment to stop. Both informal and formal methods of resolving problems should be available.

Employees should be advised that, if possible, they should attempt to resolve the problem informally in the first instance. In some cases, it may be possible and sufficient for the employee to explain clearly to the person engaging in the unwanted conduct that the behaviour in question is not welcome, that it offends them or makes them uncomfortable, and that it interferes with their work.

In circumstances where it is too difficult or embarrassing for an individual to do this on their own behalf, an alternative approach would be to seek support from, or for an initial approach to be made by, a sympathetic friend or confidential counsellor.

If the conduct continues or if it is not appropriate to resolve the problem informally, it should be raised through the formal complaints procedure.

(ii) *Advice and assistance*

It is recommended that employers designate someone to provide advice and assistance to employees subjected to sexual harassment, where possible with responsibilities to assist in the resolution of any problems, whether through informal or formal means. It may be helpful if the officer is designated with the agreement of the trade unions or employees, as this is likely to enhance their acceptability. Such officers could be selected from personnel departments or equal opportunities departments for example. In some organisations they are designated as 'confidential counsellors' or 'sympathetic friends'. Often such a role may be played by someone from the employee's trade union or women's support groups.

Whatever the location of this responsibility in the organisation, it is recommended that the designated officer receives appropriate training in the best means of resolving problems and in the detail of the organisation's policy and procedures, so that they can perform their role effectively. It is also important that they are given adequate resources to carry out their function, and protection against victimisation for assisting any recipient of sexual harassment.

(iii) *Complaints procedure*

It is recommended that, where the complainant regards attempts at informal resolution as inappropriate, where informal attempts at resolution have been refused, or where the outcome has been unsatisfactory, a formal procedure for resolving the complaint be provided. The procedure should give employees confidence that the organisation will take allegations of sexual harassment seriously.

By its nature sexual harassment may make the normal channels of complaint difficult to use because of embarrassment, fears of not being taken seriously, fears of damage to reputation, fears of reprisal or the prospect of damaging the working environment. Therefore, a formal procedure should specify to whom the employee should bring a complaint, and it should also provide an alternative if in the particular circumstances the normal grievance procedure may not be suitable, for example because the alleged harasser is the employee's line manager. It is also advisable to make provision for employees to bring a complaint in the first instance to someone of their own sex, should they so choose.

It is good practice for employers to monitor and review complaints of sexual harassment and how they have been resolved, in order to ensure that their procedures are working effectively.

(iv) *Investigations*

It is important to ensure that internal investigations of any complaints are handled with sensitivity and with due respect for the rights of both the complainant and the alleged harasser. The investigation should be seen to be independent and objective. Those carrying out the investigation should not be connected with the allegation in any way, and every effort should be made to resolve complaints speedily — grievances should be handled promptly and the procedure should set a time limit within which complaints will be processed, with due regard for any time limits set by national legislation for initiating a complaint through the legal system.

It is recommended as good practice that both the complainant and the alleged harasser have the right to be accompanied and/or represented, perhaps by a representative of their trade union or a friend or colleague; that the alleged harasser be given full details of the nature of the complaint and the opportunity to respond, and that strict confidentiality be maintained throughout any investigation into an allegation. Where it is necessary to interview witnesses, the importance of confidentiality should be emphasised.

It must be recognised that recounting the experience of sexual harassment is difficult and can damage the employee's dignity. Therefore, a complainant should not be required repeatedly to recount the events complained of where this is unnecessary.

The investigation should focus on the facts of the complaint and it is advisable for the employer to keep a complete record of all meetings and investigations.

(v) *Disciplinary offence*

It is recommended that violations of the organisation's policy protecting the dignity of employees at work should be treated as a disciplinary offence and the disciplinary rules should make clear what is regarded as inappropriate behaviour at work. It is also good practice to ensure that the range of penalties to which offenders will be liable for violating the rule is clearly stated and also to make it clear that it will be considered a disciplinary offence to victimise or retaliate against an employee for bringing a complaint of sexual harassment in good faith.

Where a complaint is upheld and it is determined that it is necessary to relocate or transfer one party, consideration should be given, wherever practicable, to allowing the complainant to choose whether he or she wishes to remain in their post or be transferred to another location. No element of penalty should be seen to attach to a complainant whose complaint is upheld and in addition, where a complaint is upheld, the employer should monitor the situation to ensure that the harassment has stopped.

Even where a complaint is not upheld, for example because the evidence is regarded as inconclusive, consideration should be given to transferring or rescheduling the work of one of the employees concerned rather than requiring them to continue to work together against the wishes of either party.

6. RECOMMENDATIONS TO TRADE UNIONS

Sexual harassment is a trade union issue as well as an issue for employers. It is recommended as good practice that trade unions formulate and issue clear policy statements on sexual harassment and take steps to raise awareness of the problem of sexual harassment in the workplace, in order to help create a climate in which it is neither condoned or ignored. For example, trade unions could aim to give all officers and representatives training on equality issues, including dealing with sexual harassment, and include such information in union-sponsored or approved training courses, as well as information on the union's policy. Trade unions should consider declaring that sexual harassment is inappropriate behaviour and educating members and officials about its consequences is recommended as good practice.

Trade unions should also raise the issue of sexual harassment with employers and encourage the adoption of adequate policies and procedures to protect the dignity of women and men at work in the organisation. It is advisable for trade unions to inform members of their right not to be sexually harassed at work and provide members with clear guidance as to what to do if they are sexually harassed, including guidance on any relevant legal rights.

Where complaints arise, it is important for trade unions to treat them seriously and sympathetically and ensure that the complainant has an opportunity of representation if a complaint is to be pursued. It is important to create an environment in which members feel able to raise such complaints knowing they will receive a sympathetic and supportive response from local union representatives. Trade unions could consider designating specially trained officials to advise and counsel members with complaints of sexual harassment and act on their behalf if required. This will provide a focal point for support. It is also a good idea to ensure that there are sufficient female representatives to support women subjected to sexual harassment.

It is recommended too, where the trade union is representing both the complainant and the alleged harasser for the purpose of the complaints procedure, that it be made clear that the union is not condoning offensive behaviour by providing representation. In any event, the same official should not represent both parties.

It is good practice to advise members that keeping a record of incidents by the harassed worker will assist in bringing any formal or informal action to a more effective conclusion, that the union wishes to be informed of any incident of sexual harassment and that such information will be kept confidential. It is also good practice for the union to monitor and review the union's record in responding to complaints and in representing alleged harassers and the harassed, in order to ensure its responses are effective.

7. EMPLOYEES' RESPONSIBILITIES

Employees have a clear role to play in helping to create a climate at work in which sexual harassment is unacceptable. They can contribute to preventing sexual harassment through an awareness and sensitivity towards the issue and by ensuring that standards of conduct for themselves and for colleagues do not cause offence.

Employees can do much to discourage sexual harassment by making it clear that they find such behaviour unacceptable and by supporting colleagues who suffer such treatment and are considering making a complaint.

Employees who are themselves recipients of harassment should, where practicable, tell the harasser that the behaviour is unwanted and unacceptable. Once the offender understands clearly that the behaviour is unwelcome, this may be enough to put an end to it. If the behaviour is persisted in, employees should inform management and/or their employee representative through the appropriate channels and request assistance in stopping the harassment, whether through informal or formal means.

COMMISSION RECOMMENDATION (87/567/EEC)

of 24 November 1987

on vocational training for women

THE COMMISSION OF THE EUROPEAN COMMUNITIES,

Having regard to the Treaty establishing the European Economic Community and the second indent of Article 155 thereof,

Whereas Article 4 of Directive 76/207/EEC of 9 February 1976 on the implementation of the principle of equal treatment for men and women as regards access to employment, vocational training and promotion, and working conditions (¹) lays down that the Member States shall ensure application of the principle of equal treatment with regard to access to all types and to all levels of vocational training and retraining;

Whereas the Commission communication to the Council transmitted on 20 December 1985, on equal opportunities for women — medium-term community programme 1986 to 1990, included education and training as one of the seven fields of action defined therein and stated that the Commission will propose Community guidelines on vocational training for women;

Whereas the second Council Resolution of 24 July 1986 on the promotion of equal opportunities for women (²) supported the broad outlines of the Commission communication referred to above and supported the programme's objectives of realising in practice equal opportunities in economic, social and cultural life;

Whereas the second Council Resolution also called on Member States to take appropriate action on the basis of, *inter alia,* the Commission communication;

Whereas Council Decision 86/365/EEC of 24 July 1986 adopting the programme on cooperation between universities and enterprises regarding training in the field of technology (Comett) (³), Council Decision 87/327/EEC of 15 June 1987 adopting the European action scheme for the mobility of university students (Erasmus) (⁴), the Resolution of the Council and the Ministers for Education meeting within the Council of 12 July 1982 concerning measures to be taken to improve the preparation of young people for work and to facilitate their transition from education to working life (⁵), the Resolution of the Council and the Ministers for Education meeting within the Council of 3 June 1985, containing an action programme on equal oppor-

tunities for girls and boys in education(⁶), the proposals for a Council decision adopting an action programme for the training and preparation of young people for adult and working life (⁷), and the Commission communication on adult training in firms(⁸), have all underlined the importance to be attached to equal opportunities;

Whereas the European Parliament has on several occasions emphasised the need for a comprehensive large-scale policy in the area of equal opportunities for women and has urged the promotion of adequate vocational training for women;

Whereas the need for well-targeted vocational training measures has been heightened by the fact that the structural crisis on the labour market and the introduction of the new technologies have seriously affected women's employment prospects and whereas the demographic trend and the economic and social changes call for the skills of all workers to be more closely attuned to requirements;

Whereas this situation has led to the development in the Member States of various initiatives designed to promote more appropriate skills for women but whereas the measures involved have often remained limited; whereas certain measures have also been undertaken at Community level and whereas the European Social Fund contributes to the financing of vocational training operations;

Whereas it is therefore important to establish Community guidelines for carrying out a number of specific comprehensive actions in a variety of fields in order to develop appropriate vocational training for women,

RECOMMENDS AS FOLLOWS:

Article 1

It is recommended that the Member States should adopt a policy designed to encourage the participation of young and adult women in training schemes, especially those relevant to occupations of the future, and should develop specific measures, particularly as regards training, for occupations where women are under-represented.

(¹) OJ L 39, 14.1.1976, p. 40.
(²) OJ C 203, 24.7.1986, p. 2.
(³) OJ L 222, 8.8.1986, p. 17.
(⁴) OJ L 166, 25.6.1987, p. 20.
(⁵) OJ C 193, 28.7.1982, p. 1.

(⁶) OJ C 166, 5.7.1985, p. 1.
(⁷) COM(87) 90 final.
(⁸) COM(86) 780.

Article 2

It is recommended that the Member States should introduce, continue or encourage active measures designed to:

(a) integrate training for women within a broader process of cooperation between all the parties concerned: the education authorities and oganisations, school and vocational guidance, the two sides of industry, the training organisations, the lenders of capital, the central and/or regional and/or local authorities, equal opportunities organisations, undertakings, women's groups or associations;

(b) staff the guidance, training and placement services with persons qualified to deal with the specific problems of women (e.g. equal opportunities counsellors) and to take measures to increase the awareness of instructors;

(c) reorganize the school, university and vocational guidance services in such a way that they seek out rather than wait to be approached by the people concerned;

(d) encourage the participation of women and girls in training courses by providing more decentralised and more widely distributed education and training facilities;

(e) develop awareness and information measures so as to offer women and those around them images of women engaged in non-traditional activities, particularly those related to occupations of the future;

(f) encourage the participation of girls in higher education, particularly in technical and technological fields, by:

— making provision within the grants system for ways of compensating for the double sexual and social handicap borne by girls from underprivileged backgrounds,

— adopting measures enabling girls to benefit on an equal footing from the programmes set up in the context of the links to be developed between universities and industry (in particular the Comett programme) and from inter-university agreements promoting the mobility of students (particularly the Erasmus programme),

— making efforts to steer girls towards key areas of new technology;

(g) encourage greater participation by girls in the various initial vocational training systems outside the education system, especially apprenticeships, other than those teaching certain 'female' occupa-

tions and adapt or, where appropriate, abolish types of training for women which do not provide real occupational skills or lead girls into overcrowded occupations;

(h) encourage girls and women to set up their own businesses or cooperatives by introducing special training and further training schemes particularly designed to provide:

— training in financial management,

— information on access to back-up and financial facilities;

(i) develop measures designed to promote the participation of women in continuous training entailing:

— campaigns to provide information and promote awareness of the potential offered by such training,

— measures to encourage women to follow such training courses, for example by adapting the conditions of training courses (e.g. timetables, duration and forms of training) to the specific problems of women and, where appropriate, by setting target figures, to be reviewed, particularly for sectors and occupations where women are under represented;

(j) provide specific courses for certain categories of women, particularly underprivileged women and women returning to work after an interruption, particularly in the confidence-building, awareness or pre-training phases;

(k) open up all types of training (paticularly those intended for unemployed people) to women wishing to return to work and encourage the two sides of industry to develop 'reintegration' projects providing training likely to enable the persons in question to re-enter the firm at the level at which they left;

(l) enable the spouses of self-employed workers who help with that self-employed activity to take advantage of training opportunities on the same terms as self-employed workers;

(m) introduce support measures such as the provision of flexible childminding arrangements and the establishment of the appropriate social infrastructures so as to enable mothers to take part in training schemes, the introduction of financial incentives or the payment of allowances during training;

(n) recognise skills acquired in running a household and looking after a family (exemption for certain course elements, etc);

(o) monitor the progress of women having taken part in training schemes, particularly in occupations where women are underrepresented.

Article 3

The Member States shall inform the Commission within three years of the date of this Recommendation of the measures taken to give effect to it, in order to allow the Commission to draw up a report on all such measures.

Article 4

This Recommendation is addressed to the Member States.

Done at Brussels, 24 November 1987.

For the Commission
Manuel MARÍN
Vice-President

Council resolutions

COUNCIL RESOLUTION (97/C 394/01)

of 4 December 1997

concerning the report on the state of women's health in the European Community

THE COUNCIL OF THE EUROPEAN UNION,

Referring to the Commission report of 19 July 1995 on the state of health in the European Community and the Council's conclusions of 30 November 1995 ([1]);

Recalling that, in the aforementioned conclusions, the Council considered that the preparation of reports containing comprehensive and accurate information on health status, determinants of health and health-related activities throughout the Community provides a way in which to help improve public knowledge and understanding of major health problems in the Community and of the action and programmes being undertaken at Community and Member State level;

Recalling also that in the said conclusions the Council agreed to consider further the objective and format of future reports, the sources of data to be used, the frequency of their publication and how they might be used as a basis for determining priorities for Community action;

Welcomes the Commission's report of 22 May 1997 on the state of women's health in the European Community;

Observes that this report highlights a lack of reliable, up-to-date and comparable data as well as a lack of data broken down according to gender;

Notes that this report shows a considerable increase in women's life expectancy since 1970 and continuing differences between the life expectancy of women in the different Member States and between the life expectancy of men and that of women;

Notes also that the report highlights sexual and reproductive health problems, the increase in breast and lung cancers, the problem of violence against women with its adverse impact on physical and psychological health, the high number of attempted suicides, the different aspects of eating disorders and the extent of chronic illnesses resulting from women's increased life expectancy;

Considers that the specific problems linked to women's health should be taken into account when the new framework for action in the field of public health is being considered;

Considers that, for the purposes of drawing up future reports,

— the objective of the reports should be to provide information on health trends and determinants which can be used in the planning, among other things, of measures to be undertaken at Community level as well as for the evaluation of those already being carried out,

— topics should be selected according to their significance for future Community measures in the field of health,

— these reports should take account of the socioeconomic factors affecting health, analyse in greater depth, in the fields considered, the data and the differences between Member States and their causes, and, where appropriate, formulate operational conclusions for action at Community level;

Stresses that Member States should be consulted in advance and the competent authorities/bodies of the Member States associated with the preparation of these reports, including the validation of data;

Emphasises that the actions to be implemented under the programme of Community action on health monitoring within the framework for action in the field of public health (1997 to 2001) ([2]) are aimed, *inter alia,* at establishing Community indicators by developing appropriate methods for collecting health data rendered progressively more comparable, as well as support for analyses and reports on health status, trends and determinants;

Considers that this work, carried out in close cooperation with the Member States, is an essential contribution towards improving the quality and comparability of the data so as to increase the reliability of the reports;

Considers that this work will also contribute towards the definition of an appropriate methodology for preparing future reports and the improvement of their quality and value;

Calls upon the Member States to proceed with the breakdown of health data by gender, account being taken of socioeconomic factors, and to gather more data concerning health problems specific to women, paying particular attention to improving women's

([1]) OJ C 350, 30.12.1995, p. 1.

([2]) Decision No 1400/97/EC of the European Parliament and of the Council of 30 June 1997 (OJ L 193, 22.7.1997, p. 1).

quality of life, given *inter alia* the increase in women's life expectancy;

Calls upon the Commission to:

— take due account of this report in implementing the programmes under way and in developing future action, including determining the priorities for Community action,

— attach particular importance to improving the quality and comparability of health data and to their breakdown according to gender in the framework of the programme of Community action on health monitoring,

— for the preparation of future reports, consult the Member States in an appropriate manner, in particular in the committee for the health monitoring programme, in order to determine the objective and format of future reports, the frequency with which they should appear, the choice of topics, the data sources to be used, the methods to be followed and the selection of coordinators.

———

COUNCIL RESOLUTION (96/C 386/01)

of 2 December 1996

on mainstreaming equal opportunities for men and women into the European Structural Funds

THE COUNCIL OF THE EUROPEAN UNION,

(1) Whereas equal opportunities for men and women on the labour market also promote competitiveness and economic growth; whereas the mainstreaming of equal opportunities into structural policies is a response to the need to reduce inequality of opportunities between men and women with regard to the rate of employment, the level of training, access to the labour market and involvement in the decision-making process;

(2) Whereas the Heads of State or Government meeting within the European Council at Madrid on 15 and 16 December 1995 reaffirmed that the fight against unemployment and for equal opportunities is the priority task of the European Union and its Member States, and agreed that there should be an intensification of efforts to promote equal opportunities in the field of employment;

(3) Whereas the European Structural Funds (ERDF, ESF, EAGGF and FIFG) constitute an important instrument for working towards this goal, in accordance with their legal and economic commitments;

(4) Whereas the priority objectives of the Structural Funds are governed by Council Regulation (EEC) No 2052/88 of 24 June 1988 on the tasks of the Structural Funds and their effectiveness and on coordination of their activities between themselves and with the operations of the European Investment Bank and the other existing financial instruments [1] and each of the Funds contributes in appropriate fashion to them; whereas the differences between the Funds must be respected if they are to achieve those objectives;

(5) Whereas Regulation (EEC) No 2052/88 clearly sets down the respective responsibilities of the Member States and of the Commission in the implementation of the Structural Funds, in the framework of partnership and in accordance with the principle of subsidiarity;

(6) Whereas Regulations (EEC) No 2081/93 [2], No 2082/93 [3], No 2083/93 [4], No 2084/93 [5] and No 2085/93 [6] governing the Structural Funds adopted by the Council in 1993 refer to the principle of equal opportunities for men and women on the employment market as a goal to which structural measures should contribute; whereas promoting equal opportunities on the labour market is a specific task of the European Social Fund;

(7) Whereas the medium-term Community action programme on equal opportunities for men and women (1996 to 2000), adopted by the Council under Decision 95/593/EC [7], is intended to promote the integration of equal opportunities for men and women in the process of preparing, implementing and monitoring all policies and activities of the European Union and the Member States, having regard to their respective powers;

(8) Whereas the mainstreaming of equal opportunities for men and women into all policies and activities is one of the key principles set out in the Platform for Action adopted by the Fourth World Conference on Women (Beijing, 14 and 15 September 1995);

(9) Whereas, in spite of the improvements made since the adoption of the Council Resolution of 22 June 1994 on the promotion of equal opportunities for men and women through action by the European Structural Funds [8], Structural Fund operations to promote equal opportunities could be further improved, and efforts to mobilise the various partners involved and in particular the national and regional authorities responsible for devising and implementing the programmes must be continued and intensified, as noted in the Communication from the Commission of 21 February 1996 on incorporating equal opportunities for women and men into all community policies and activities;

(10) Whereas this point was endorsed at the European conference on equal opportunities and the Structural Funds held in Brussels on 7 and 8 March 1996 at the initiative of the Belgian Government;

(11) Whereas a more active approach to economic and social solidarity, with particular emphasis on measures to promote equal opportunities for men and women, should be promoted; whereas the

---

[1] OJ L 185, 15.7.1988, p. 9. Regulation as last amended by Regulation (EC) No 3193/94 (OJ L 337, 24.12.1994, p. 11).
[2] OJ L 193, 31.7.1993, p. 5.
[3] OJ L 193, 31.7.1993, p. 20.
[4] OJ L 193, 31.7.1993, p. 34.
[5] OJ L 193, 31.7.1993, p. 39.
[6] OJ L 193, 31.7.1993, p. 44.
[7] OJ L 335, 30.12.1995, p. 37.
[8] OJ C 231, 20.8.1994, p. 1.

Funds might play an important role in reconciling family and working life and in integrating disadvantaged women and this can be combined with local employment initiatives and with the development of new sources of employment, as noted in the Communication from the Commission of 20 March 1996 on Community structural assistance and employment;

(12) Whereas further impetus should be given towards mainstreaming equal opportunities into action supported by the Structural Funds, in the light of recent developments and commitments at the highest level and in view of forthcoming reviews;

(13) Whereas the monitoring committees have an essential role to play in ensuring that the aims affirmed in the programming of all Structural Funds will receive practical expression in the implementation process; whereas they should work to ensure that the mainstreaming of equal opportunities into the Structural Funds is translated into concrete measures,

I. CALLS ON THE COMMISSION AND THE MEMBER STATES, WORKING IN PARTNERSHIP AND HAVING REGARD TO THEIR RESPECTIVE COMPETENCES, to make a continued, deepened and determined effort to mainstream the principle of equal opportunities for men and women into action supported by the Structural Funds.

II. CALLS ON THE MEMBER STATES:

1. in accordance with the provisions laid down in the Regulations and with the priorities and commitments agreed in the Community Support Frameworks and in the single programming documents, to promote strengthened use of the Structural Funds to support actions which will make a positive contribution to the promotion of equal opportunities, in such areas, for instance, as the improvement of social infrastructure, access to employment and the terms and conditions of employment, access to business services and facilities, and the reconciliation of professional and family life for women and men;

2. to make full use of the existing programming possibilities of the various forms of Structural Fund intervention to promote equal opportunities, where appropriate by undertaking more operations combining the use of the different Structural Funds for actions in promotion of equal opportunities;

3. to examine the scope for refocussing programmes in response to the priorities established by the European Council at Essen and confirmed at Cannes and Madrid, namely the fight against unemployment and for equal opportunities.

III. CALLS ON THE COMMISSION AND THE MEMBER STATES, WORKING IN PARTNERSHIP AND HAVING REGARD TO THEIR RESPECTIVE COMPETENCES:

1. in relation to monitoring:

    (a) to ensure, where appropriate, the participation in the monitoring committees of the competent authorities and bodies involved in promoting equal opportunities at local, regional and national level;

    (b) to promote a balanced participation of women and men in the decision-making, selecting and monitoring bodies at local, regional and national level;

    (c) to ensure, where appropriate, regular consideration of equal opportunities by the monitoring committees, with a view to examining how efforts to promote equal opportunities within the mainstream of Structural Fund actions and Community initiatives, as well as through specific initiatives, can be improved;

    (d) to cooperate in the production of statistics, on the basis of available data, which are an essential prerequisite for measuring:

    — the impact of action supported by the Structural Funds on the availability of social infrastructure,

    — break down of long-term unemployed by sex,

    — female and male economic activity rates, and

    — proportions of women and men by socioeconomic category;

    (e) to consider using the flexibility which results from annual reprogramming of unspent credits to strengthen efforts to promote equal opportunities;

2. in relation to evaluations and forthcoming reviews:

    (a) to ensure that evaluations measure the extent to which the principle of promoting equal opportunities has been taken into account in the current programming period, with particular regard to the involvement of women in general measures and to the implementation, the relevance and the outcome of such measures; to develop, where appropriate, adequate evaluation procedures, tools and indicators to this end;

(b) on the basis of these evaluations, to decide on any changes which it may be necessary to make in the programming of actions for the remainder of the programming period.

IV. INVITES THE COMMISSION:

1. on the basis of existing structures, to systematise:

   — the identification of good practice with regard to the promotion of equal opportunities through action supported by the various Structural Funds, and

   — the dissemination of information and experience on such good practice;

2. to take account of this resolution, as well as the Council Resolution of 22 June 1994 on the promotion of equal opportunities for men and women through action by the European Structural Funds, when making a proposal for review by the Council of the Structural Funds;

3. to review each year in its annual report on the Structural Funds the impact of this Resolution, beginning with the report drawn up in 1998.

RESOLUTION OF THE COUNCIL AND OF THE REPRESENTATIVES OF THE GOVERNMENTS OF THE MEMBER STATES, MEETING WITHIN THE COUNCIL (95/C 296/06)

of 5 October 1995

on the image of women and men portrayed in advertising and the media

THE COUNCIL OF THE EUROPEAN UNION AND THE REPRESENTATIVES OF THE GOVERNMENTS OF THE MEMBER STATES, MEETING WITHIN THE COUNCIL,

Whereas the Council resolution of 12 July 1982 on the promotion of equal opportunities for women [1] confirms the need to take steps to increase public awareness and disseminate information to support the change in attitudes to sharing occupational, family and social responsibilities;

Whereas the European Parliament resolution of 14 October 1987 on the depiction and position of women in the media [2] recommends the media, advertising agencies, governments and socio-political groups to implement practical measures to encourage the promotion of women, guarantee equal opportunities and define the role played by women in professional, political and social life;

Whereas Council Directive 89/552/EEC of 3 October 1989 on the coordination of certain provisions laid down by law, regulation or administrative action in Member States concerning the pursuit of television broadcasting activities [3] stipulates that television advertising should not jeopardise respect for human dignity or include any discrimination on grounds of sex;

Whereas the Commission, in its third medium-term action programme on equal opportunities for women and men (1991 to 1995), has defined actions to promote a positive image of women, emphasising in particular the promotion of a better representation of women in the media industry as well as in the institutional and professional environment of media organisations, the development of innovatory programmes which challenge traditional images and the drawing up of recommendations concerning the representation of women in the media industry;

Whereas the Council, in its resolution of 21 May 1991 on the third medium-term Community action programme on equal opportunities for women and men (1991 to 1995) [4], invited the Member States to continue to encourage an improvement in the participation of women at all levels in the media sector and to develop innovatory programmes which present a full, realistic picture of women in society;

Whereas the Council, in its resolution of 27 March 1995 on the balanced participation of men and women in decision-making [5], invited Member States to promote the balanced participation of women and men in decision-making as a priority objective in the context of their respective practices regarding equal opportunities for women and men;

Whereas the European Council, at its meetings in Essen (9 and 10 December 1994) and Cannes (26 and 27 June 1995), stressed that questions concerning equal opportunities for women and men are among those that will continue to constitute the most important tasks of the European Union and its Member States;

Whereas the European Conference of Women Ministers of the Member States of the Council of Europe (Brussels, 7 March 1994) declared its wish to achieve genuine equality between men and women in the Europe of tomorrow, came out in favour of promoting an image of women and men that was positive and free of prejudices or stereotypes and insisted on the need to implement all possible measures, e. g. a code of ethics, to prevent discrimination against women;

Whereas advertising and the media could play a part in changing attitudes in society by reflecting in particular the diversity of the roles played by both women and men in public and private life; whereas the roles of women in public life are represented less than those of men; whereas the roles of men in private life are represented much less often than those of women;

Whereas this resolution does not affect national respective constitutional rules or approaches and practices;

Whereas the Member States and/or the respective competent bodies must take into account the differences between advertising — even that in the media — and the media themselves as a forum for information and debate,

I. CONFIRM:

    1. their attachment to the principle of freedom of expression and to the principle of freedom of the press and other means of communication;

[1] OJ C 186, 21.7.1982, p. 3.
[2] OJ C 305, 16.11.1987, p. 66.
[3] OJ L 298, 17.10.1989, p. 23.
[4] OJ C 142, 31.5.1991, p. 1.

[5] OJ C 168, 4.7.1995, p. 3.

2. that sexual stereotyping in advertising and the media is one of the factors in inequality which influence attitudes towards equality between women and men; that this highlights the importance of promoting equality in all areas of social life;

3. that advertising and the media can play an important part in changing attitudes in society by reflecting the diversity of the roles and potential of women and men, their participation in all aspects of social life, as well as a more balanced sharing of family, occupational and social responsibilities between women and men;

4. that advertising and the media should not undermine respect for human dignity nor contain discrimination on grounds of sex;

II. CALL ON the Member States and/or the respective competent bodies, in compliance with their national constitutional rules and/or approaches and practices to:

1. promote a diversified and realistic picture of the skills and potential of women and men in society;

2. take action aimed at disseminating this image by implementing measures with a view to:

2.1. providing for appropriate measures to ensure respect for human dignity and an absence of discrimination on grounds of sex;

2.2. implementing and/or encouraging regular information and awareness campaigns to promote awareness in advertising agencies, the media and the public so that they can identify material which is discriminatory on grounds of sex and is conveyed by advertising and the media;

2.3. supporting and/or promoting forums for discussion, consultation, monitoring — where appropriate within a framework of voluntary

self-regulation — and follow-up with regard to material which is discriminatory on grounds of sex and is conveyed by advertising and the media;

2.4. supporting studies and initiatives which increase awareness in advertising agencies and the media of equality of opportunity and a more balanced sharing of responsibilities, in particular in public, political, economic, professional, social and family life;

2.5. placing special importance on values connected with equality of opportunity in all its forms and at all levels of education and training, particularly training for professions in advertising and the media;

2.6. promoting the balanced participation of women and men in production bodies, administrative bodies and decision-making posts;

2.7. encouraging advertising agencies and the media to promote:

(a) the study, creation and formulation of new ideas to reflect the diversity of the roles of women and men;

(b) recognition of the negative effects which stereotypes based on sex may have on the physical and mental health of the public in general and of young people in particular;

(c) the development and implementation of voluntary self-regulatory codes;

III. CALL ON the Commission to:

1. take account of this resolution, in particular when implementing its action programmes for equal opportunities for women and men;

2. establish and/or strengthen contacts with the bodies and organisations, at European level, specialised in the field of advertising and the media, and with the social partners.

COUNCIL RESOLUTION (95/C 168/02)

of 27 March 1995

on the balanced participation of men and women in decision-making

THE COUNCIL OF THE EUROPEAN UNION,

Whereas, in its third medium-term action programme on equal opportunities for men and women (1991 to 1995), the Commission undertook to develop Community action in a new key area concerning the participation of women in the decision-making process at every level of society, in order to improve the status of women in society;

Whereas the Council confirmed its support for the overall objective of this third action programme in its resolution of 21 May 1991 (¹): it invited the Member States to 'encourage measures designed to promote the participation of women in the decision-making process in public, economic and social life';

Whereas the Council invited both sides of industry to 'take all necessary measures actively to promote women's representation in decision-making bodies';

Whereas, in its resolution of 11 February 1994 on women in decision-making bodies, the European Parliament invited the Member States to undertake specific action in this area;

Whereas the European Conference of Women Ministers from the Member States of the Council of Europe (Brussels, 7 March 1994) proclaimed, in its declaration of principle, its determination to bring about genuine equality between men and women in the Europe of tomorrow;

Whereas the first European conference on women in power (Athens, 2 and 3 November 1992) in particular highlighted the fact that the under-representation of women in decision-making prevents full account being taken of the interests and needs of the population as a whole,

1. AFFIRMS THAT:

   (a) the objective of balanced participation of men and women in decision-making and the sharing of responsibilities between men and women in every sphere of life constitutes an important condition for equality between men and women;

   (b) it is necessary to make every effort to bring about the changes in structures and attitudes which are essential for genuine equality of access to decision-making posts for men and

women in the political, economic, social and cultural fields;

2. INVITES the Member States to:

   (a) promote the balanced participation of men and women in decision-making as a priority objective in the context of their respective practices regarding equal opportunities for men and women and to adopt this objective as such in their governments' programmes;

   (b) develop an integrated global strategy for promoting the balanced participation of men and women in decision-making which spans the broad range of the following measures and takes into account the options and best methods applied in the various Member States;

      (i) regularly compiling and publishing a report containing figures on the participation of women in decision-making posts in the political, economic, social and cultural fields, in order to acquire accurate knowledge of the factual situation and to promote awareness;

      (ii) developing incentives and support measures for non-governmental organisations in general and in particular for groups who are actively committed in the field to this objective;

      (iii) developing support for scientific research in this area so as to permit the development of new ideas and concepts;

      (iv) devising, launching and promoting information and awareness campaigns at regular intervals, designed to fuel public debate and to develop more progressive outlooks as regards both the general public and specific target groups;

      (v) instigating and accompanying initiatives, setting examples and opening up the way in practice in the various areas of decision-making and thereafter developing programmes designed to generalise effective action;

      (vi) developing an appropriate framework, where necessary encompassing specific measures, and encouraging the balanced participation of men and women in decision-making in the political, economic, social and cultural fields;

(¹) OJ C 142, 31.5.1991, p. 1.

3. CALLS UPON the institutions and bodies of the European Communities:

    (a) to implement measures, in their capacity as employers and on the basis of a review, promoting the balanced recruitment of men and women and, *inter alia,* by promotion and training actions, enabling balanced participation in decision-making duties to be achieved;

    (b) to evaluate the results thereof periodically and have them published;

4. CALLS UPON the Commission:

    (a) to step up its information and awareness effort and its efforts to promote research and to introduce pilot schemes to implement the balanced participation of men and women in decision-making;

    (b) — to take account of this resolution in its fourth action programme on equal opportunities for men and women;

    — to draw up, taking account of that fourth action programme, a draft recommendation to be submitted to the Council aimed at promoting the balanced participation of men and women in decision-making;

    (c) to ensure that the Member States are kept informed regularly on progress made in this area;

5. CALLS UPON both sides of industry to step up their efforts to ensure the balanced participation of men and women in decision-making bodies;

6. RECALLS the discussions held and the initiatives taken within the Council in the past on the topics dealt with in this resolution;

7. UNDERTAKES TO conduct regular discussions on the topics covered by this resolution.

RESOLUTION OF THE COUNCIL AND OF THE REPRESENTATIVES OF THE GOVERNMENTS OF THE MEMBER STATES MEETING WITHIN THE COUNCIL (94/C 368/02)

of 6 December 1994

on equal participation by women in an employment-intensive economic growth strategy within the European Union

THE COUNCIL OF THE EUROPEAN UNION AND THE REPRESENTATIVES OF THE GOVERNMENTS OF THE MEMBER STATES MEETING WITHIN THE COUNCIL,

Having regard to the Treaty establishing the European Community,

Whereas the Council directives on equal treatment for men and women have made an essential contribution to improving the position of women;

Whereas Directives 75/117/EEC ([1]), 76/207/EEC ([2]), 79/7/EEC ([3]) and 86/613/EEC ([4]) adopted with a view to harmonising the living and working conditions of men and women and promoting equal treatment of men and women are of considerable importance in this context;

Whereas the Community action programmes on equal opportunities for women and men covering the periods 1982 to 1985, 1986 to 1990 and 1991 to 1995, together with the undertakings entered into in this context and in several related areas, constitute positive contributions to promoting equality of opportunity;

Whereas implementation of the principle of equal pay for equal work or work of the same value provided for in Article 119 of the Treaty as well as of the resulting principle of equality, in accordance with Community provision, is an essential feature of the construction and operation of the common market;

Whereas the harmonisation of the living and working conditions of men and women is essential in the interests of equitable economic and social development; whereas, at its meetings in Madrid and Strasbourg, the European Council stressed the need to pay as much attention to economic and social aspects;

Whereas earlier efforts made in particular in the areas of awareness, education and training and the aid available under the European Social Fund have created conditions favourable to the pursuit of more ambitious future objectives;

Whereas, pursuant to Article 2 of the Treaty, one of the tasks of the Community is to promote a high level of employment;

Whereas provision should be made, while respecting the responsibilities of Member States and bearing in mind the characteristics of the labour market structure in each Member State, including the different types of work, for a sufficient supply of full-time and/or part-time work for both men and women;

Whereas an effective policy of equal opportunities presupposes an integrated, overall strategy allowing for better organisation of working hours and greater flexibility, and for an easier return to working life; whereas a strategy of this type must cover qualification opportunities targeted at women and the promotion of self-employment,

I

1. Recall that the legal instruments of the Community constitute the necessary basis for the development of Community action, and emphasise the role of the Commission as the guardian of the Treaties;

2. Stress that:

   (a) equal opportunities depend on men and women being able to support themselves by taking up paid employment;

   (b) Europe needs a high level of skills;

   (c) current demographic trends already suggest that the growing number of highly educated women provides a hitherto insufficiently exploited source of skills and innovative capacity which will have to be developed and used more intensively;

   (d) the female unemployment rate in most Member States far exceeds the rate for men, particularly where long-term unemployment is concerned;

   (e) while the level of female employment has risen in recent years at Union level, women are still over-represented in the less skilled and lower paid jobs which offer less security and are concentrated in a small number of employment sectors;

([1]) OJ L 45, 19.2.1975, p. 19.
([2]) OJ L 39, 14.2.1976, p. 40.
([3]) OJ L 6, 10.1.1979, p. 24.
([4]) OJ L 359, 19.12.1986, p. 56.

(f) women are under-represented in management posts and in new areas of employment requiring a high level of technical skills;

(g) women wishing to join the labour market face specific structural and practical difficulties;

3. Confirm that if the internal market is to continue to develop dynamically and notably if new jobs are to be created, positive measures in particular will have to be taken to promote equal opportunities between men and women;

4. Put forward against this background a number of important objectives without wishing to foreclose discussion within the Union:

(a) facilitating access by women to the labour market and their progress up the career ladder, in particular by improving opportunities to gain qualifications;

(b) overcoming the sex-based segregation of the labour market;

(c) promoting the employment of women in decision-making posts in economic, social and political circles and institutions, with the aim of achieving equal employment;

(d) removing the discrepancy between men's and women's pay;

(e) promoting full-time and part-time work on a voluntary basis;

(f) improving the organisation and flexibility of working hours;

(g) promoting self-employment, and, in particular the creation and recovery of businesses;

Improving the flexibility of working hours

5. Note, while acknowledging the important role and responsibilities of the two sides of industry in this area, that improving the organisation and flexibility of working hours within the framework of an active employment policy:

(a) is both a necessity as regards commercial management and the national economy and a social requirement which will offer both men and women an opportunity to reconcile their work responsibilities with their family obligations and personal interests;

(b) must be underpinned by adequate structures, such as child-care services;

(c) can have positive implications for employment;

6. Are concerned that the labour market is segregated on the basis of sex, particularly in the area of part-time work;

7. Believe, to this end, that it is necessary to:

(a) introduce flexibility of working hours into working arrangements in both the public and the private sectors;

(b) make flexible working arrangements possible in a growing number of areas of employment, qualified jobs, as far as possible, included;

(c) use the increased flexibility of working hours in such a way as to have a positive effect on employment;

(d) organise part-time work on a voluntary basis for men and women in order to break down the sex-based segregation of the labour market;

(e) instruct personnel managers in the organisation of working time and in questions involving work preoccupations, with a view to encouraging equal opportunities;

Europe needs a high level of skills

8. Note that:

(a) new technologies presuppose a high level of skills on the part of workers; it is precisely these technologies which require a basic level of training which can be built on, and continuing training;

(b) the number of training posts available remains largely based on sex and, together with the sex-based obstacles which inhibit access to work and to career advancement, continues to prevent any extension of the range of jobs open to women;

9. Stress that if women are to be ready to meet future challenges and to develop their potential in a wide range of jobs at all levels, it is essential that:

(a) greater numbers of women be given training in non-traditional jobs, particularly technical ones, and have an improved chance of finding work;

(b) women be prepared for positions of responsibility and for new sectors of employment, in particular in the technical sphere, by means of specific measures which will provide young women with role models;

(c) the traditionally female jobs be modernised and upgraded and the possibilities for promotion improved;

(d) the training and vocational training possibilities offered be better tailored to the needs of women within an adequate structural framework (e.g. childcare) and continuing career and professional development planning encouraged;

(e) women be offered specific further training which will open up new career prospects to them, particularly in rural areas particularly affected by structural change;

(f) women benefit adequately from national and Community assistance measures, taking into account the proportion of women in all target groups (e.g. young people without training, the unemployed, the long-term unemployed);

(g) national and transnational strategies designed to combine activities to improve vocational training and the job opportunities for women receive effective support at various levels with a view to putting into practice new prospects and innovations, particularly within undertakings;

Facilitating the continued entry and re-entry of women into the labour market

10. Stress that it is therefore advisable to

(a) maintain the flow of women into the labour market, and

(b) facilitate their return to work after a career break for family reasons by offering opportunities for guidance and retraining;

Encouraging self-employment

11. Note that:

(a) in a number of Member States a considerable proportion of businesses are started up by women, and that the creation and recovery of businesses by women can have a positive effect on employment;

(b) for many women, setting up a business means escaping from unemployment while at the same time creating jobs for others;

12. Are convinced that, consequently:

(a) business creation or recovery programmes should take particular account of the specific needs of women and offer them relevant opportunities for guidance;

(b) the conditions laid down in business creation or recovery programmes should be examined to see whether they would be equally relevant to action in the services sector;

(c) chambers of commerce, banks, administrative bodies and local authorities:

— should cooperate to pinpoint needs and the possibilities on offer for guidance and retraining so that women who wish to create or recover a business are able to do so, particularly in the framework of new job-

creation measures in regions where development has lagged behind,

— should take account of the fact that many women set up businesses gradually (for instance, beginning as a side-line);

II

1. INVITE THE MEMBER STATES to:

(a) develop policies for reconciling the obligations of family and work, including measures to encourage and facilitate greater involvement by men in domestic life;

(b) recognise that, apart from the general aim of a high level of employment, measures aimed at promoting the flexibility of working hours, encouraging voluntary part-time work and improving the skills level and their support for the creation or recovery of businesses, as outlined by the Commission in its White Paper on growth, competitiveness and employment, must for the sake of equal treatment, be of benefit to women as well as men;

(c) make use of the discussions held on the implementation of the said White Paper to increase the integration of policies to help women into the economic, financial, social and labour-market policies of the Union and its Member States while at the same time developing new actions thanks to specific programmes aimed at women and giving effective support to interdisciplinary strategies;

(d) support the Commission in its preparation of the fourth programme of Community medium-term action for equal opportunities for women and men from 1996 to 2000;

(e) take full account of the responsibilities and powers of both sides of industry in this area;

2. INVITE THE TWO SIDES OF INDUSTRY to:

(a) hold collective bargaining on the subject of equal opportunities and equal treatment by endeavouring in particular to ensure that, in undertakings and in the various occupational sectors, the introduction and organisation of flexible working hours and voluntary part-time work and the return to work are facilitated;

(b) ensure that women are adequately represented on in-service training courses in undertakings;

(c) continue and step up the social dialogue on how work and family responsibilities are to be reconciled as well as on the problem of protecting the dignity of men and women at the work place;

106

(d) press during collective bargaining for equal pay and the abolition of discrimination based on sex — where it exists — in pay or job-classification scales;

(e) take all necessary steps to increase the representation of women on decision-making bodies;

3. INVITE THE COMMISSION:

(a) in preparation for the fourth action programme on equal opportunities for women and men (1996 to 2000):

— to take a fresh, closer look at the objective of equality between men and women with an eye to an employment-intensive economic growth strategy,

— to develop initiatives designed to improve flexibility, promote part-time work and the acquisition of new skills or qualifications and encourage the creation or recovery of businesses;

(b) when drawing up and implementing the policies and action programmes in the employment field, to ensure that the goals of equality of opportunity and equal treatment continue to take priority, and pursue with greater intensity the action already initiated.

COUNCIL RESOLUTION (94/C 231/01)

of 22 June 1994

on the promotion of equal opportunities for men and women through action by the European Structural Funds

THE COUNCIL OF THE EUROPEAN UNION,

1. Recalls that the principle of equal opportunities for men and women on the labour market is an objective of the European Union and that structural action must contribute to the achievement of that objective, within the meaning of Council Regulation (EEC) No 2052/88 of 24 June 1988 on the tasks of the Structural Funds and their effectiveness and on coordination of their activities between themselves and with the operations of the European Investment Bank and the other existing financial instruments (¹);

2. Recalls that the adoption of measures intended to support the promotion of equal opportunities for men and women on the labour market shall be undertaken in accordance with the responsibility of Member States arising from the rules in force concerning the Structural Funds;

3. Recalls that the promotion of equal opportunities for men and women on the labour market is one of the four measures under Objective 3 throughout the European Union, as provided for in Article 1 (1) (d) of Council Regulation (EEC) No 4255/88 of 19 December 1988 laying down provisions for implementing Regulation (EEC) No 2052/88 as regards the European Social Fund (²);

4. Recalls that women experience serious and particular difficulties in the labour market;

5. Confirms its wish that the declared principle of equal opportunities for men and women should be promoted, in particular through all the structural measures taken in the Member States;

6. Invites the Member States:

(a) to contribute towards ensuring that due account is taken of promoting the principle of equal opportunities for men and women on the labour market in measures co-financed by the European Structural Funds, in particular the European Social Fund;

(b) to contribute to the adoption of appropriate measures to support the promotion of equal opportunities for men and women on the labour market in the measures financed by the European Structural Funds so as to enable women to take advantage of the prospective benefits on an equal footing with men;

(c) to help to ensure that specific measures targeted at women are laid down with appropriate financial appropriations with the aim of improving the position of women, and to promote at local, regional, national and transnational level, equal opportunities for men and women in every sector of economic activity and in all areas linked directly or indirectly to the labour market, by making use, in particular, of the achievements of the Community initiative NOW;

(d) to use every appropriate means to inform, mobilise and encourage competent bodies and social and economic partners, within the meaning of Article 4 (1) of Regulation (EEC) No 2052/88, so that full account is taken of the dimension of equal opportunities for men and women in measures co-financed by the European Structural Funds;

(e) to use every appropriate means to define and promulgate the policy of promoting equal opportunities for men and women through the action of the European Structural Funds;

(f) to help to ensure that the present point is implemented, within the existing national monitoring and assessment structures.

7. Invites the Commission:

(a) to continue its efforts to put into effect the policy of promoting equal opportunities for men and women through action by the European Structural Funds, in particular by the European Social Fund and Community initiatives;

(b) to facilitate implementation of this policy by means of technical assistance, in particular within the framework of the principle of partnership;

(c) to take all appropriate measures to further this policy;

(d) to take account of the objectives mentioned in point 6 when implementing Community initiatives.

(¹) OJ L 185, 15.7.1988, p. 9. Regulation as amended by Council Regulation (EEC) No 2081/93 (OJ L 193, 31.7.1993, p. 5).
(²) OJ L 374, 31.12.1988, p. 21. Regulation as amended by Council Regulation (EEC) No 2084/93 (OJ L 193, 31.7.1993, p. 39).

COUNCIL RESOLUTION (91/C 142/01)

of 21 May 1991

on the third medium-term Community action programme on equal opportunities for women and men (1991 to 1995)

THE COUNCIL OF THE EUROPEAN COMMUNITIES,

Having regard to the Treaties establishing the European Communities,

Whereas the Directives adopted by the Council in the area of equal treatment for men and women have played an important role in improving the situation of women;

Whereas the Community Charter of the Fundamental Social Rights of Workers, adopted at the Strasbourg European Council meeting on 9 December 1989 by the Heads of State or Government of 11 Member States, and in particular point 16 thereof, declared that:

'Equal treatment for men and women must be assured. Equal opportunities for men and women must be developed.

To this end, action should be intensified to ensure the implementation of the principle of equality between men and women as regards in particular access to employment, remuneration, working conditions, social protection, education, vocational training and career development.

Measures should also be developed enabling men and women to reconcile their occupational and family obligations.';

Whereas the 1982 to 1985 and 1986 to 1990 action programmes and the undertakings given in this framework, together with those adopted in related areas, constitute positive contributions to the promotion of equal opportunities;

Whereas the efforts undertaken, particularly with regard to raising awareness, to information and training, and the assistance provided under the European Social Fund have prepared the way for future achievements on a larger scale;

Whereas, in spite of the efforts made at Community level and notwithstanding an improvement in the economic situation, inequalities nevertheless continue to exist, especially with regard to the employment of women;

Whereas the completion of the internal market is the most effective way of creating employment, ensuring maximum well-being in the Community and providing better opportunities for a qualified work-force on the labour market;

Whereas there is a dual need to consolidate the work already undertaken within the framework of the two previous action programmes regarding equal opportunities and to develop new policies and measures taking into account the social and economic changes of the 1990s and beyond;

Whereas women must be in a position to benefit on equal terms from the achievement of the single market and to contribute fully to such achievement; whereas, in order to meet the challenges of the 1990s, better use should be made of women's abilities and gifts so as to permit their full participation in the process of European development and a re-valuing of their contribution to that process; whereas that participation is an essential factor in European economic and social cohesion;

Whereas an overall, integrated approach is necessary in order to implement an effective policy of equal opportunities for women and men;

Whereas the two sides of industry have a very important role to play in the implementation of the third medium-term Community action programme on equal opportunities for women and men (1991 to 1995),

HEREBY ADOPTS THIS RESOLUTION:

I

THE COUNCIL:

— recalls that Community legal instruments constitute the necessary basis for the development of Community action and stresses the role of the Commission as the guardian of the Treaties,

— underlines that this basis can be strengthened by the adoption of other Community legal instruments,

— confirms that the efforts already undertaken should be intensified and developed with a view to:

— improving the implementation of existing legal provisions,

— promoting the integration of women on the labour market,

— improving the status of women in society,

— notes the Commission communication on a third medium-term Community action programme on equal opportunities for women and men (1991 to 1995) and supports the overall objective of that programme,

— recognises the need to adopt an overall integrated approach allowing the policies on equality to be given full effect,

— confirms that it is therefore advisable to:

— strengthen cooperation between all the parties concerned in the implementation of this programme in order to achieve a policy of true partnership between the Commission, the Member States, regional and local authorities and the two sides of industry,

— intensify the social dialogue regarding equality,

— integrate the objective of equal opportunities and equal treatment in the formulation and implementation of the relevant policies and action programmes at both Community and Member State level and, to that end, apply more efficiently and, if necessary, improve institutional arrangements at Member State level, to enable equal opportunities and equal treatment to be effectively achieved in all areas.

II

THE COUNCIL:

1. INVITES THE MEMBER STATES

to implement the relevant measures provided for in the Commission communication on a third medium-term community action programme on equal opportunities for women and men (1991 to 1995), in order to achieve the following objectives:

— ensure the implementation and, if necessary, improvement of existing legal provisions; raise the level of awareness about legal rights and obligations,

— increase the participation of women in the labour market by applying national laws and practices in an improved manner to women, by developing specific measures for equal opportunities for women and men, and by promoting women's entrepreneurship and local employment initiatives,

— improve the quality of women's employment by maximising their potential, particularly

through stepping up action relating to education, vocational training, better staff management and the use of positive action in enterprises,

— reduce barriers to women's access to, and participation in, employment, also through measures designed to reconcile the family and occupational responsibilities of both women and men,

— continue, and develop, awareness-raising initiatives which are related to the specific objectives of this programme, and improve and disseminate information on equal opportunity and equal treatment issues,

— continue to encourage an improvement in the participation of women at all levels in the media sector and to develop innovatory programmes which present a full, realistic picture of women in society,

— encourage measures designed to promote the participation of women in the decision-making process in public, economic and social life.

2. INVITES THE MEMBER STATES:

— to adopt, as required, within the framework of this programme, national, regional or local equality plans or other relevant policy measures establishing objectives that match national circumstances,

— to draw up assessment reports,

given that collaboration and complementarity of measures between Member States and the Commission are essential in order to achieve the objectives of this programme.

3. INVITES BOTH SIDES OF INDUSTRY TO:

— make equal opportunities and equal treatment an element in collective bargaining, in particular by endeavouring to implement positive action programmes in undertakings and in occupational branches and sectors as part of a cohesive policy of staff management and to elicit a real commitment to in-service training and jobs for women,

— pursue and intensify the social dialogue on the issues of reconciling occupational and family responsibilities and protecting the dignity of women and men at work,

— include in collective bargaining the issues of equal remuneration (equal pay for equal work or work of equal value) and the elimination of discrimination on the basis of sex in job assessment and/or classification,

— take all necessary measures actively to promote women's representation in decision-making bodies.

4. INVITES THE COMMISSION TO:

— ensure that the present programme is implemented and make interim and overall assessments (at mid-term and at the end of the period) of the policy on equal opportunities and equal treatment, on the basis of the information supplied by the Member States, taking into account all action carried out by the Commission and outlining the action carried out by the Member States,

— submit the results of these assessments to the European Parliament, the Council and the Economic and Social Committee,

— integrate the objective of equal opportunities and equal treatment into the formulation and implementation of the appropriate policies and action programmes and introduce specific means of coordination.

COUNCIL RESOLUTION (90/C 157/02)

of 29 May 1990

on the protection of the dignity of women and men at work

THE COUNCIL OF THE EUROPEAN COMMUNITIES,

Having regard to the Treaty establishing the European Economic Community,

Whereas unwanted conduct of a sexual nature, or other conduct based on sex affecting the dignity of women and men at work, including the conduct of superiors and colleagues, is unacceptable and may, in certain circumstances, be contrary to the principle of equal treatment within the meaning of Articles 3, 4 and 5 of Council Directive 76/207/EEC of 9 February 1976 on the implementation of the principle of equal treatment for men and women as regards access to employment, vocational training and promotion, and working conditions [1], a view supported by case-law in some Member States;

Whereas, in accordance with the Council recommendation of 13 December 1984 on the promotion of positive action for women [2], many Member States have carried out a variety of positive action measures and actions having a bearing, *inter alia,* on respect for the dignity of women at the workplace;

Whereas the European Parliament, in its resolution of 11 June 1986 on violence against women [3], has called upon national authorities to strive to achieve a legal definition of sexual harassment and has called upon national governments, equal opportunities committees and trade unions to carry out concerted information campaigns to create a proper awareness of the individual rights of all members of the labour force;

Whereas the Council is anxious to take account of the study which found that sexual harassment is a serious problem for many working women in the European Community and is an obstacle to the proper integration of women into the labour market [4];

Whereas the Advisory Committee on Equal Opportunities between Women and Men, in its opinion of 20 June 1988, has unanimously recommended that there should be a recommendation and code of conduct on sexual harassment in the workplace covering harassment of both sexes,

1. AFFIRMS, that conduct of a sexual nature, or other conduct based on sex affecting the dignity of women and men at work, including conduct of superiors and colleagues, constitutes an intolerable violation of the dignity of workers or trainees and is unacceptable if:

(a) such conduct is unwanted, unreasonable and offensive to the recipient;

(b) a person's rejection of, or submission to, such conduct on the part of employers or workers (including superiors or colleagues) is used explicitly or implicitly as a basis for a decision which affects that person's access to vocational training, access to employment, continued employment, promotion, salary or any other employment decisions;

and/or

(c) such conduct creates an intimidating, hostile or humiliating work environment for the recipient;

2. CALLS ON the Member States to:

1. develop campaigns of information and awareness for employers and workers (including superiors and colleagues), taking account of the best practice which exists in various Members States, to counter unwanted conduct of a sexual nature or other conduct based on sex affecting the dignity of women and men at work;

2. promote awareness that the conduct described in paragraph 1 may be, in certain circumstances, contrary to the principle of equal treatment within the meaning of Articles 3, 4 and 5 of Council Directive 76/207/EEC;

3. remind employers that they have a responsibility to seek to ensure that the work environment is free from:

(a) unwanted conduct of a sexual nature or other conduct based on sex affecting the dignity of women and men at work;

(b) victimisation of a complainant or of a person wishing to give, or giving, evidence in the event of a complaint;

4. develop appropriate positive measures in accordance with national legislation in the public sector which may serve as an example to the private sector;

---

[1] OJ L 39, 14.2.1976, p. 40.
[2] OJ L 331, 19.12.1984, p. 34.
[3] OJ C 176, 14.7.1986, p. 79.
[4] 'The dignity of women at work — Report on the problem of sexual harassment in the Member States of the European Communities, October 1987' (ISBN 92-825-8764-9).

5. consider that both sides of industry, while respecting their autonomy and subject to national traditions and practices, could examine in the context of the collective bargaining process the question of including appropriate clauses in agreements, aimed at achieving a work environment as described in paragraph 3;

3. CALLS ON the Commission to:

1. continue its efforts to inform and make aware employers, workers (including superiors and colleagues), lawyers and members of courts, tribunals and other competent authorities of the importance of the concept set out in paragraph 1 and of the fact that, in certain circumstances, failure to respect this concept may be contrary to the principle of equal treatment within the meaning of Articles 3, 4 and 5 of Directive 76/207/EEC;

2. draw up, by 1 July 1991, in consultation with both sides of industry and following consultation with the Member States and national equal opportunities authorities, a code of conduct on the protection of the dignity of women and men at work which will provide guidance, based on examples and best practice in the Member States, on initiating and pursuing positive measures designed to create a climate at work in which women and men respect one another's human integrity.

4. CALLS ON the institutions and organs of the European Communities also to:

1. respect the concept set out in paragraph 1;

2. develop positive action measures aimed at achieving a work environment as described in paragraph 2 (3).

COUNCIL RESOLUTION (88/C 333/01)

of 16 December 1988

on the reintegration and late integration of women into working life

THE COUNCIL OF THE EUROPEAN COMMUNITIES,

Having regard to the Treaty establishing the European Economic Community,

Whereas a considerable number of women give up work on marriage or on childbirth on account of the difficulty of reconciling their working life and family life; whereas many young women are not integrated into working life, in particular for family reasons;

Whereas women who wish to return to work or make a late entry into employment often encounter problems and could become long-term unemployed;

Whereas the labour market offers better opportunities for skilled labour; whereas many women who wish to return to work or make a late entry into employment do not have the qualifications to do so;

Whereas some Member States have carried out research/measures to support the return of women to work;

Whereas the reintegration and late integration of women into working life is a problem throughout the Community, which also requires solutions at Community level;

Whereas all Community citizens must benefit from the large internal market; whereas the implementation of the social dimension of the internal market necessitates effective measures for the reintegration and late integration of women into working life,

HEREBY ADOPTS THIS RESOLUTION:

I. The Council calls on the Member States to take the following measures:

1. build up information on the labour market situation, especially on occupations which do not offer many prospects of employment and occupations which will be in demand in the future, in particular those connected with new technology;

2. ensure that the staff of guidance, training and placement services are qualified to deal with the specific problems of women who wish to return to work or make a late entry into employment (hereinafter referred to as 'the women concerned');

3. ensure that the women concerned enjoy the best conditions, in so far as those conditions are applicable, of access to vocational training and integration into working life;

4. organise, where appropriate in cooperation with both sides of industry, vocational training programmes or other measures which meet the specific needs of the women concerned;

5. promote measures with a view to helping women during preparation for reintegration or late integration into working life, in particular to build up their self-confidence and develop their basic technical skills;

6. promote measures to monitor closely the reintegration and late integration of women during a transitional period, so as to ensure that reintegration and late integration do not end in failure;

7. encourage as far as possible child-minding initiatives organised in a way which takes account of the professional situation of parents and appropriate initiatives to assist disabled and elderly persons in order to lessen the family responsibilities of the women concerned;

8. encourage steps designed to see that breaks in women's careers are accompanied by appropriate measures, for example maintaining skills or keeping up contacts between them and their former employers, *inter alia* with a view to possible reintegration;

9. develop cooperation between national, regional and local authorities, women's organisations, organisers of training programmes and other interested bodies;

10. build up quantitative and qualitative data enabling all the problems and needs of the women concerned to be identified as far as possible.

II. The Council calls on the Commission to take the following measures:

1. consolidate the studies carried out in the Member States in the field of the reintegration and late integration of women into working life;

2. list and evaluate the measures taken in the Member States in this field;

3. take account of the women concerned when compiling Community statistics;

4. take account, within the rules of the European Social Fund, of measures for the reintegration and late integration of women into working life;

5. encourage vocational training measures and pilot programmes to help the women concerned;

6. facilitate the exchange of experience between Member States regarding the measures taken by them for the benefit of the women concerned, and disseminate information concerning those measures;

7. forward to the Council, on the basis of the information supplied by the Member States, a report on the implementation of this Resolution not later than five years after its adoption.

SECOND COUNCIL RESOLUTION (86/C 203/02)

of 24 July 1986

on the promotion of equal opportunities for women

THE COUNCIL OF THE EUROPEAN
COMMUNITIES,

Having regard to the Treaties establishing the European Communities,

Having regard to the draft resolution submitted by the Commission ([1]),

Having regard to the opinion of the European Parliament ([2]),

Having regard to the opinion of the Economic and Social Committee ([3]),

Whereas, in order to promote equal opportunities for women, various measures have been taken at Community level, in particular the adoption by the Council of Directive 75/117/EEC of 10 February 1975 on the approximation of the laws of the Member States relating to the application of the principle of equal pay for men and women ([4]), Directive 75/207/EEC of 9 February 1976 on the implementation of the principle of equal treatment for men and women as regards access to employment, vocational training and promotion, and working conditions ([5]) and Directive 79/7/EEC of 19 December 1978 on the progressive implementation of the principle of equal treatment for men and women in matters of social security ([6]);

Whereas these Community legal instruments constitute the basis needed for the development of Community action;

Whereas the 1982 to 1985 action programme and the commitments entered into in that connection, in particular the Council resolution of 12 July 1982 concerning the promotion of equal opportunities for women ([7]), the Council resolution of 7 June 1984 on action to combat unemployment amongst women ([8]) and the Council recommendation of 13 December 1984 on the promotion of positive action for women ([9])

and those adopted in certain related areas ([10]), constitute positive contributions to the promotion of equal opportunities;

Whereas, however, inequality persists and seems likely to increase in the present economic climate;

Whereas efforts already under way must be intensified and developed with a view to achieving genuine equality, so that women can approach social, technological and occupational change on an equal footing with men;

Whereas the European Parliament has frequently urged the need for a comprehensive and wide-ranging policy to promote equal opportunities for women;

Whereas it should be noted with approval that the Commission firmly believes that the programme's objective of realising in practice equal opportunities in economic, social and cultural life can and should be achieved without imposing any unreasonable burden on the economy and undertakings;

Considering the conclusions of the European Council of 2 and 3 December 1985 on the matter,

1. Points to the directives, recommendations, resolutions and other instruments adopted concerning the promotion of equal opportunities for women;

2. Recalls the proposals for directives already submitted by the Commission, and agrees to continue its efforts to seek solutions to the problems involved;

3. Confirms the need to develop and intensify action at Community and national level through a systematic and coherent wide-ranging policy designed to eliminate *de facto* inequalities, whatever the

---

([1]) OJ C 356, 31.12.1985, p. 28.
([2]) Opinion delivered on 13 May 1986 (not yet published in the Official Journal).
([3]) Opinion delivered on 24 April 1986 (not yet published in the Official Journal).
([4]) OJ L 45, 19.2.1976, p. 19.
([5]) OJ L 39, 14.1.1976, p. 40.
([6]) OJ L 6, 10.1.1979, p. 24.
([7]) OJ C 186, 21.7.1982, p. 3.
([8]) OJ C 161, 21.6.1984, p. 4.
([9]) OJ L 331, 19.12.1984, p. 34.

([10]) Particularly:
— Council resolution of 2 June 1983 concerning vocational training measures relating to new information technologies (OJ C 166, 25.6.1983, p. 1),
— Council resolution of 11 July 1983 concerning vocational training policies in the European Community in the 1980s (OJ C 193, 20.7.1983, p. 2),
— Resolution of the Council and the Ministers for Education meeting within the Council of 19 September 1983 on measures relating to the introduction of new information technology in education (OJ C 256, 24.9.1983, p. 1),
— Council resolution of 23 January 1984 on the promotion of employment for young people (OJ C 29, 4.2.1984, p. 1),
— Resolution of the Council and the Ministers for Education meeting within the Council of 3 June 1985 containing an action programme on equal opportunities for girls and boys in education (OJ C 166, 5.7.1985, p. 1).

economic situation, and to promote genuine equality of opportunity;

4. Supports the broad outlines of the Commission communication concerning a new medium-term programme on equal opportunities for women (1986 to 1990) and supports that programme's objective of realising in practice equal opportunities in economic, social and cultural life; reiterates in this context, the importance of promoting job creation;

5. Calls on the Member States to take appropriate action on the basis of, *inter alia,* the elements of the Commission communication referred to in point 4 of this resolution and in particular to:

— ensure effective application of existing equal-treatment legislation, particularly through the systematic provision of information, the development of suitable mechanisms to carry through and prepare provisions on equal treatment, and the examination of all aspects of the problems relating to the establishment of proof in this regard,

— develop comprehensive and coordinated action in the fields of education and training in order to create a better balance between men and women in the various types of teaching establishment and to widen career choices to include sectors and trades of the future, in particular those concerned with new technologies, enterprise creation and self-employed occupations, in accordance with the resolution of 3 June 1985,

— adopt adequate measures to increase the number of women in jobs linked to the introduction of new technologies, with a view to promoting desegregation and as a response to the resulting changes,

— develop and intensify specific action promoting the employment of women and, in particular, support local initiatives and adopt measures to ensure that women have equal opportunities to set up businesses, particularly cooperatives, as well as measures to support self-employed women, including those working in agriculture,

— adopt a more systematic policy to promote the presence of both sexes in employment at all levels, particularly through the development of positive action in all fields, the revision of protective legislation which is no longer justified and the search for specific solutions for the most disadvantaged categories,

— review social-protection and social-security provisions, taking into account the changing place of women in employment,

— develop measures to encourage the sharing of family and career responsibilities through measures to increase awareness and steps to adapt and reorganise working time, with due regard for the responsibilities of both sides of industry, development of the social infrastructure, particularly child-minding facilities, and of adequate solutions for groups and persons who particularly need them,

— launch or encourage at all appropriate levels systematic and wide-ranging information and awareness campaigns to highlight the positive aspects of equality, thereby promoting a change in attitudes, especially through the media and by targeting a variety of groups, in order to reach all participants in political, social, occupational and educational life, particularly women themselves,

— encourage both sides of industry to take steps to secure effective equality of opportunity and efficacy of positive measures at the workplace,

— actively promote greater participation by women in the public and private sectors, particularly in posts for responsibility, and in decision-making bodies;

6. Will continue to promote consistency between specific measures to promote equal opportunities and overall economic and social policy at both Community and national level and instructs the Commission to keep a check on the consistency of its measures at Community level while encouraging positive action to help women within the limits of the means available and avoiding any measure which might discourage women from joining the job market;

7. Agrees to develop more systematic cooperation on Member States' policies and actions on equal treatment, and instructs the Commission to organise such cooperation with all bodies concerned, such as national authorities, equal-treatment bodies and committees, both sides of industry;

8. Requests the Commission to prepare a progress report and an assessment of the implementation of this programme by 1 January 1991 and accordingly invites the Member States to forward the necessary information to the Commission before 1 January 1990.

RESOLUTION (85/C 166/01) OF THE COUNCIL AND OF THE MINISTERS FOR EDUCATION, MEETING WITHIN THE COUNCIL,

of 3 June 1985

containing an action programme on equal opportunities for girls and boys in education

THE COUNCIL AND THE MINISTERS FOR EDUCATION, MEETING WITHIN THE COUNCIL,

Having regard to the Treaties establishing the European Communities,

Having regard to the resolution of the Council and of the Ministers for Education, meeting within the Council, of 9 February 1976 comprising an action programme in the field of education [1],

Having regard to Council Directive 76/207/EEC of 9 February 1976 on the implementation of the principle of equal treatment for men and women [2] and in particular Article 2 (4) and Articles 3 and 4 thereof,

Having regard to the Council resolutions and those of the Council and of the Ministers for Education, meeting within the Council, dealing with equal opportunities for women [3][4][5][6][7],

Having regard to the Council Recommendation 84/635/EEC of 13 December 1984 on the promotion of positive action for women [8],

Having regard to the various European Parliament resolutions in favour of women [9], and in particular the resolution of 17 January 1984 [10] on the situation of women in Europe,

Bearing in mind that educational establishments are a particularly suitable forum for effective action to achieve equal opportunies for girls and boys;

Whereas education and vocational training are among the prerequisites for achieving equal opportunities for men and women in working life and whereas education should therefore contribute to eradicating stereotypes, encourage acceptance of the principles of fair sharing of family and occupational responsibilities and prepare young people adequately for working life;

Bearing in mind the importance of involving all participants in the educational process in implementation of any policy to foster equal opportunities in order to achieve the necessary change in mentalities and attitudes;

Whereas the decisive influence of parents is widely recognised in connection with stereotype-formation, the perception of social roles of men and women and also as regards the duration of schooling and educational and career choices;

Bearing in mind the commitment of teachers and their associations to the achievement of equal opportunities for girls and boys in the school system;

Whereas, in addition to policies concerning equal access for girls and boys to all forms and levels of education, positive action is necessary to bring about equality in practice;

Taking note of the report of the conference on equality of opportunity for girls and boys in education (Brussels, 27 and 28 November 1984), organised by the Presidency in conjunction with the Commission,

HEREBY ADOPT THIS RESOLUTION:

I

The Council and the Ministers for Education, meeting within the Council, give their agreement to an action programme which will be implemented within the scope of constitutional possibilities and having regard to the economic, social and cultural context of each Member State, to the funds available and to their respective educational systems. The measures envisaged under this programme are necessary in order to:

— ensure equal opportunities for girls and boys for access to all forms of education and all types of training in order to enable each individual to develop his or her own aptitudes to the full;

— enable girls and boys to make educational and career choices, in full knowledge of the facts and in good time, affording them the same

---

[1] OJ C 38, 19.2.1976.

[2] OJ L 39, 14.2.1976.

[3] Resolution on the promotion of equal opportunities for women (OJ C 186, 21.7.1982).

[4] Resolution concerning vocational training measures relating to new information technologies (OJ C 166, 25.6.1983).

[5] Resolution concerning vocational training policies in the European Community in the 1980s (OJ C 193, 20.7.1983).

[6] Resolution on measures relating to the introduction of new information technology in education (OJ C 256, 24.9.1983).

[7] Resolution on action to combat unemployment amongst women, and in particular section II(b) thereof (OJ C 161, 21.6.1984).

[8] OJ L 331, 19.12.1984.

[9] OJ C 50, 9.3.1984 and OJ C 149, 14.6.1982.

[10] OJ C 50, 9.3.1984.

possibilities as regards employment and economic independence;

— motivate girls and boys to make non-traditional choices and to follow courses leading to qualifications so that they may have access to a far more diversified range of jobs;

— encourage girls to participate as much as boys in new and expanding sectors, within both education and vocational training, such as the new information technologies and biotechnology.

The Council and the Ministers for Education, meeting within the Council, accordingly agree that these objectives can be attained if the educational and career choices of girls and boys are made without any restriction as to sex.

The action programme is as follows:

1. *Promoting awareness among all the participants in the educational process* (¹) *of the need to achieve equal opportunities for girls and boys*

    (a) Encouraging the eradication of sex stereotyping through coordinated action to raise awareness such as information campaigns, seminars, lectures, debates and discussions;

    (b) encouraging exchanges of information on innovatory projects in this field and ensuring that it is as widely disseminated as possible;

    (c) preparing and distributing at national level texts bringing together results of experience, recommendations and practical guidance aimed at achieving equal opportunities.

2. *Educational and vocational guidance as a service to all pupils to encourage girls and boys to diversify their career choices*

    (a) Ensuring that information is given as early as possible on working life and delay the introduction of options, since premature specialisation leads to a preference for traditional course options and maintains segregation;

    ensuring that information, counselling and guidance services are available to all pupils throughout their school career and in particular at all the key points at which course options are decided;

    making it possible to switch courses during the school career, e.g. by means of bridging classes;

    (b) encouraging diversification of girls' and boys' educational and career choices, particularly by:

        — introducing both girls and boys to new technology from the end of primary school in all educational establishments,

        — training guidance officers in the specific aspects of educational and career guidance relating to girls (encouraging diversity of choice, in particular new careers connected with new technologies, and providing follow-up and support for girls who take non-traditional options, etc.),

        — ensuring effective cooperation between school guidance services and parents and teachers as well as between school and vocational guidance, training and job-vacancy services.

3. *Opening up schools to working life and the outside world,* in particular by organising, at all levels, pupil contact with working life, especially where non-traditional work for women is being promoted, and with the outside world in general (associations of young people, occupational bodies, etc.).

4. *Extending the possibilities for effective access by both girls and boys to all vocational training options and supporting, through suitable measures, girls and boys who have chosen non-traditional openings.*

5. *Including the question and pedagogics of equal opportunity in teachers' initial and in-service training.* Teachers' courses could for instance include the components needed to encourage girls to take up the natural sciences and mathematics, and information on the vocational opportunities offered by these disciplines.

6. *Reinforcing co-educational practices in mixed educational establishments*

    In mixed educational establishments encouraging all pupils to participate in school and extra-mural activities, including activities traditionally considered as being either for the male or female sex and stimulate in particular equal participation by girls and boys in technical and scientific options.

7. *Developing a balance between men and women holding positions of responsibility in education*

    Encouraging children to develop a positive perception of equality of the sexes by promoting a balanced distribution of men and women working in the educational sector; to this end, encourage action aimed at improving the balance in terms of postings, promotion and training. This improved

---

(¹) In particular, children, parents, inspectors, heads of educational establishments, teacher-training staff, teachers, educational counsellors, guidance officers, local authorities.

balance should cover both the subjects taught and the levels of the posts occupied.

8. *Eradicating persistent stereotypes from school textbooks, teaching material in general, assessment materials and guidance material*

   (a) Creating structures or using existing structures for equal opportunities for girls and boys with a view to establishing criteria and drawing up recommendations aimed at eliminating stereotypes from school books and all other teaching and educational material, with involvement of all the parties concerned (publishers, teachers, public authorities, parents' associations);

   (b) encouraging gradual replacement of material containing stereotypes by non-sexist material.

9. *Special measures helping the underprivileged,* particularly girls who receive very little encouragement from their families to pursue school activities and the children of migrant workers (prevention of illiteracy, language training). These measures are aimed at pupils, teachers and parents. They are particularly concerned with informing migrant workers of the educational options available in the host country.

10. *Introducing specific measures to encourage the promotion of programmes for equal opportunities for girls and boys,* with a view to:

    — encouraging the implementation in schools of specific measures based on guidelines agreed at national level;

    — drawing up annual reports on action taken;

    — encouraging the training of school advisers specifically appointed to make recommendations, give advice, suggest initiatives and assess measures taken;

    — reviewing the text of regulations (such as circulars) with a view to eradicating discrimination and stereotypes from them;

    — encouraging the use of existing agencies with expertise in matters concerning equal opportunities for girls and boys in monitoring progress in this area.

II

The Commission of the European Communities will take the necessary measures to:

— promote the principle of equality between girls and boys in all Community action and policies connected with education, training and employment policy, and in particular promote a spirit of enterprise among girls as well as boys in order to facilitate their transition from school to working life,

— extend the programme of study visits to include teacher training staff, guidance officers, inspectors and administrators with particular responsibility for equal opportunities for girls and boys at school, in order to broaden their practical and vocational experience,

— provide supplementary data, particularly through studies on equal opportunities for girls and boys in education, circulate the results and improve the exchange of information on positive action by using the Eurydice network,

— ensure close cooperation with teachers' associations organised at European level in implementing and promoting measures for equal opportunities for girls and boys,

— in collaboration with parents' associations organised at European level, launch information campaigns on the choice of school courses and the division of tasks between girls and boys and aimed at eliminating stereotypes,

— set up a Working Party composed of those having responsibility at national level for matters concerning equal opportunities for girls and boys in education and of representatives of the competent bodies (experts, equal opportunities boards) to pool Member States' experience and follow up and assess the implementation of the action programme; this Working Party to report to the Education Committee,

— support, on the basis of specific criteria (e. g. transferability to other Member States), certain action undertaken by Member States, particularly the launching of innovatory programmes or projects, and actions which foster exchanges between Member States,

— support Member States in drawing up and circulating practical recommendations aimed at achieving equal opportunities, particularly by preparing Community guidelines.

III

The Council and the Ministers for Education, meeting within the Council, call upon the Commission to give careful consideration, in the framework of the rules governing the Social Fund, to applications relating to the training of instructors and guidance counsellors undertaken in the context of positive action to ensure equal opportunities for girls and boys in education.

IV

The Council and the Ministers for Education, meeting within the Council, call upon the Education Committee to submit, in two years' time, a first progress report on action taken by the Member States and the Community to foster equal opportunities for girls and boys in education.

V

Community funding of the action outlined in section II and the extent thereof will be decided in accordance with the Community's budgetary rules and procedures.

VI

This Resolution will be forwarded to the European Parliament and to the Economic and Social Committee.

COUNCIL RESOLUTION (84/C 161/02)

of 7 June 1984

on action to combat unemployment amongst women

THE COUNCIL OF THE EUROPEAN COMMUNITIES,

Having regard to the Treaties establishing the European Communities,

Having regard to the draft resolution submitted by the Commission [1],

Having regard to the opinion of the European Parliament [2],

Having regard to the opinion of the Economic and Social Committee [3],

Whereas various actions have been taken at Community level to promote equal opportunities for women, in particular the adoption, by the Council, of Directives 75/117/EEC [4], 76/207/EEC [5] and 79/7/EEC [6], concerning equal treatment as between men and women;

Whereas the Council resolution of 12 July 1982 on the promotion of equal opportunities for women [7] emphasises in particular the need, in a period of economic crisis, to intensify action undertaken at Community and national level, by the implementation of positive measures in order to achieve equality of opportunity in practice;

Whereas the Council resolutions of 11 July 1983 concerning vocational training policies in the European Community in the 1980s [8], of 2 June 1983 concerning vocational training measures relating to new information technologies [9] and of 23 January 1984 on the promotion of employment for young people [10] provide for specific measures in favour of women;

Whereas the European Parliament has on several occasions stressed the need to develop Community measures to combat female unemployment;

Whereas female unemployment in the Community, which is noticeably higher than male unemployment, requires the adoption of appropriate measures to reduce the level of this unemployment and to improve the situation of unemployed women;

Whereas the progressive reduction of the rate of female unemployment must form part of a general reduction of unemployment;

Whereas female unemployment also has special characteristics requiring appropriate measures,

HEREBY ADOPTS THIS RESOLUTION:

I. General objectives

1. The Council takes note of the Commission communication on unemployment amongst women in the Community.

2. It notes that unemployment amongst women is a worrying aspect of the general employment situation in the Community and can only be resolved satisfactorily within the framework of a general policy designed to achieve economic recovery and employment growth. Given the particular characteristics of female unemployment, it is also necessary to make specific efforts to remove the handicaps affecting the employment of women and to promote equal opportunities on the labour market in order to reduce gradually and significantly the rate of unemployment among women.

3. It emphasises the principles which must underlie the measures to be promoted, namely:

   — the equal right of men and women to work and, by the same token, to acquire a personal income on equal terms and conditions, regardless of the economic situation,

   — the extension of equal opportunities to men and women, in particular on the labour market, in the context of measures to stimulate economic recovery and to promote employment growth,

   — the development of positive measures to correct *de facto* inequalities and thereby improve female employment prospects and promote the employment of both men and women.

II. Guidelines for action

1. The Council considers that the following guidelines for action in particular should be implemented or continued within the framework of national policies and practices:

[1] OJ C 65, 6.2.1984, p. 8.
[2] Opinion delivered on 22 May 1984 (not yet published in the Official Journal).
[3] Opinion delivered on 23 May 1984 (not yet published in the Official Journal).
[4] OJ L 45, 19.2.1975, p. 19.
[5] OJ L 39, 14.2.1976, p. 40.
[6] OJ L 6, 10.1.1979, p. 24.
[7] OJ C 186, 21.7.1982, p. 3.
[8] OJ C 193, 20.7.1983, p. 2.
[9] OJ C 166, 25.6.1983, p. 1.
[10] OJ C 29, 4.2.1984, p. 1.

(a) in respect of job creation and recruitment:

— ensure that the measures aimed at encouraging the recruitment of additional labour, especially young people, in the private sector, allow for a more balanced representation of men and women, particularly in jobs in which women are under-represented and in skilled jobs,

— focus recruitment premiums, where they exist, on the people at the greatest disadvantage on the labour market, many of whom are women,

— adopt adequate measures to promote increased representation of women, in order to achieve a better balance in the industries of the future, especially the high-technology industries,

— make efforts also in the public sector to promote equal opportunities which can serve as an example, particularly in those fields where new information technologies are being developed,

— endeavour to ensure that initiatives aimed at the reduction and re-organisation of working time make a positive contribution to the promotion of equal opportunities in the area of employment, by permitting *inter alia* greater flexibility in working hours,

— ensure that voluntary part-time work does not lead to increased sexual segregation on the labour market,

— enable women to have equal access to financial and other facilities available for the creation of businesses, particularly in the context of local initiatives to create employment, including those taken on a cooperative basis, which offer women worthwhile employment prospects and working conditions;

(b) to promote, in the fields of education, vocational training and guidance, measures with a view to:

— giving women a wider choice of jobs to enable them to participate more equitably in growth sectors and in the industries of the future,

— ensuring more appropriate qualifications for female workers particularly affected by industrial restructuring and innovation, for those from less-favoured areas, for unemployed women and those seeking to return to work,

— promoting increased representation of women in training programmes in order to achieve a better balance in those sectors where they are under-represented, especially sectors connected with the introduction of new technologies;

(c) adopt the necessary measures to ensure that placement, guidance and counselling services are staffed with skilled personnel in adequate numbers in order to provide a service based on the necessary expertise in the special problems of unemployed women;

(d) improve quantitative and qualitative information on the situation of women on the labour market and the assessment of the impact of policies to combat unemployment on the employment of women in order to be able to monitor progress in the sexual desegregation of employment and identify female unemployment trends more accurately.

2. The Council stresses the importance it attaches to the positive contribution of the European Social Fund to the implementation of these guidelines for action.

3. The Council considers that the principles and guidelines set out above should apply to action undertaken at every level, also by encouraging, where possible, both sides of industry.

4. The Council stresses the importance of accompanying measures, especially regarding social infrastructure and means of encouraging greater sharing of responsibilities in the light of the general objective of improving female employment.

5. The Council asks the Members States to develop, where appropriate in cooperation with the Commission, information campaigns aimed at encouraging the change in attitudes needed to improve equality of opportunity in employment. The Council emphasises the essential role played in this respect, and also as initiators of positive action, by national committees and bodies for the promotion of equal opportunities, which must be able to act as effectively as possible.

6. The Commission is requested to organise an annual exchange of information between Member States on measures taken under this resolution to reduce unemployment among women, and on the means of monitoring, research and assessment.

7. The Council asks the Commission to report to it at regular intervals with a view to taking stock of progress accomplished not later than three years following the adoption of this resolution.

COUNCIL RESOLUTION (82/C 186/03)

of 12 July 1982

on the promotion of equal opportunities for women

THE COUNCIL OF THE EUROPEAN COMMUNTIES,

Having regard to the Treaty establishing the European Economic Community,

Having regard to the draft resolution presented by the Commission ([1]),

Having regard to the opinion of the European Parliament ([2]),

Having regard to the opinion of the Economic and Social Committee ([3]),

Whereas various actions have already been undertaken at Community level to promote equal opportunities for women, in particular the adoption, by the Council, on the basis of Articles 100 and 235 of the Treaty establishing the European Economic Community, of Directives 75/117/EEC ([4]), 76/207/ EEC ([5]) and 79/7/EEC ([6]) concerning equal treatment for men and women;

Whereas all these actions, including those supported by the European Social Fund, have played an important part in improving the situation of women;

Whereas, despite the efforts so far made at both Community and national level, actual inequalities in employment persist and may well become worse in the present economic and social conditions;

Whereas, in a period of economic crisis, the action undertaken at Community and national level should be not only continued but also intensified, in particular in order to promote the achievement of equal opportunities in practice through the implementation of *inter alia* positive measures,

Notes the Commission communication concerning a new Community Action Programme on the promotion of equal opportunities for women (1982 to 1985), which covers 'the achievement of equal treatment by strengthening individual rights' and the 'achievement of equal opportunities in practice, particularly by means of positive action programmes';

Welcomes the initiative taken by the Commission;

Approves the general objectives of this communication, namely the stepping up of action to ensure observance of the principle of equal treatment for men and women and the promotion of equal opportunities in practice by positive measures;

Expresses the will to implement appropriate measures to achieve them;

Notes also the comments which have been made on the Commission communication by the various delegations within the Council and which reveal *inter alia* certain characteristics peculiar to national systems;

Asks the Commission to take account of them in the initiatives which it takes within the framework of its powers;

Recalls the efforts which have been and are still being made in this area in the Member States;

Notes that the Commission communication defines specific objectives and joint courses of action, most of which fall within the follow-up to the implementation of the Directives adopted by the Council in the field of equal treatment for men and women;

Considers that, with due regard to the courses of action proposed, these objectives should guide the Community and the Member States in their efforts to apply on a broader basis and to realise in practice, the principle of equal opportunities without discriminating against women whatever the economic situation obtaining;

Emphasises the importance, to this end, of strengthening or setting up national bodies for the promotion of women's employment and equal opportunities;

Recalls the responsibilities which, in the pursuit of these objectives, also devolve upon workers' and employers' organisations;

Confirms the need to take steps to increase public awareness and disseminate information to support the change in attitudes to sharing occupational, family and social responsibilities;

Asks Member States to cooperate fully with the Commission in steps to increase public awareness;

Reaffirms the need to promote the employment of both men and women in all sectors and occupations and a more balanced representation of women at different levels of responsibility at both national and Community level;

([1]) OJ C 22, 29.1.1982, p. 7.
([2]) OJ C 149, 14.6.1982, p. 54.
([3]) OJ C 178, 18.7.1982, p. 22.
([4]) OJ L 45, 19.2.1975, p. 19.
([5]) OJ L 39, 14.2.1976, p. 40.
([6]) OJ L 6, 10.1.1979, p. 24.

Considers that the public sector, including the Community institutions and bodies, should set an example in this respect;

Underlines the desirability of avoiding special rules for the protection of women on the labour market and eliminating such rules in cases where originally well-founded concern for their protection is no longer justified;

Considers that account should be taken of the equal-opportunities dimension in preparing and implementing Community policies likely to affect it;

Asks the Commission to present an interim report by 1 January 1984 on progress achieved and on implementation under the new programme, based in particular on information obtained from the Member States, together with, if appropriate, suitable proposals;

Asks the Member States to send a first report to the Commission by 1 January 1985 on progress accomplished at national level; Notes the undertaking by the Commission to present an initial survey of the action undertaken before the end of 1985.

Council conclusions

CONCLUSIONS OF THE COUNCIL AND THE MINISTERS OF EDUCATION MEETING WITHIN THE COUNCIL (90/C 162/05)

of 31 May 1990

on the enhanced treatment of equality of educational opportunity for girls and boys in the initial and in-service training of teachers

THE COUNCIL AND THE MINISTERS OF EDUCATION, MEETING WITHIN THE COUNCIL,

Having regard to their resolutions concerned with the achievement of equal opportunity in education, particularly that of 3 June 1985 containing an action programme in this field[1],

Taking into account that the Commission guidelines for education and training in the medium term (1989 to 1992) place the issue of equality among the main objectives of the next phase of European educational cooperation and that the conclusions of the Council and Ministers of 6 October 1989 on cooperation and Community policy in the field of education in the run-up to 1993[2] identify equality of access to high-quality education as one of the basic elements for achieving a Europe of training,

Recognising that the extent to which educational systems effectively deal with issues of equality of opportunity is an important indicator of the quality of the systems themselves,

Reaffirming their commitment to the objective of achieving equality of opportunity for girls and boys in education,

CONCLUDE that:

— teachers have a fundamental role to play in achieving that objective,

— the nature and quality of initial and in-service training of teachers is a major factor influencing the extent to which that objective can be achieved,

— there is a need in the initial and in-service training of teachers to improve their awareness of equal opportunity in education and their skill in promoting it.

_____
[1] OJ C 166, 6.7.1985.
[2] OJ C 277, 31.10.1989.

AGREE that, within the framework of the specific educational policies and taking into account the structures of each Member State:

— the competent authorities in the Member States should review the existing provision in relation to equality of educational opportunity in teacher education courses and examine, as far as is necessary, how this question could, to a greater extent, permeate the initial and in-service training of teachers or become an integrated component of such training as appropriate,

— the development of women's studies and research on gender issues in appropriate research institutions, in particular in higher education institutions, in the Member States should be encouraged and the links between those involved in such studies and research and those responsible for the training of teachers should be strengthened,

— the training of teacher trainers within the Member States on issues related to equality of educational opportunity should be a priority area, as a means of achieving the best results within the resources available.

NOTE that, in connection with the action programme on equality, a pilot project of action research on equal opportunities in the initial and in-service training of teachers was established and that the results of it will be disseminated in due course.

CALL ON THE COMMISSION:

— to examine ways in which it can supplement and assist actions by the Member States on issues of equality of educational opportunity in the initial and in-service training of teachers,

— to arrange exchanges of information and experience between the Member States concerning examples of good practice in this field,

— to make, in collaboration with its advisory working party on equal opportunity in education, a progress report through the Education Committee to a future meeting of the Council, based *inter alia* on the experience of the Member States.

_____

COUNCIL CONCLUSIONS (87/C 178/04)

of 26 May 1987

on protective legislation for women in the Member States of the European Community

THE COUNCIL OF THE EUROPEAN COMMUNITIES,

1. notes with interest the Commission communication on protective legislation for women in the Member States of the Community, which:

— falls within the framework of the action programmes on the promotion of equal opportunities for women, and

— aims at ensuring correct application of Council Directive 76/207/EEC of 9 February 1976 on the implementation of the principle of equal treatment for men and women as regards access to employment, vocational training and promotion and working conditions [1], and in particular Article 2 (3), Article 3 (2) (c) and Article 5 (2) (c) thereof;

2. considers that the examination or revision of protective legislation for women also falls within the context of employment policy and the improvement of working conditions;

3. acknowledges that protective legislation for women must be revised where it seems detrimental to the promotion of equal opportunities for women as regards job access or ineffective in terms of the protection policy itself;

4. requests the Member States and both sides of industry to review the protective legislation for women, particularly those provisions the Commission describes as unjustified, with the aim of promoting the desegregation and more adaptable patterns of work;

5. takes note of the interpretation given by the Commission and the Court of Justice whereby exceptions to the principle of equal treatment must be assessed very restrictively, and also takes note of the opinion that the application of that principle must take place in the context of the improvement of working conditions referred to in Article 117 of the Treaty;

6. acknowledges that the improvement of working conditions, protective equipment and workers' training as well as progress in scientific knowledge are factors to be taken into account in assessing the protective provisions concerning workers' health and safety;

7. invites the Commission to update in due course its communication in conjunction with the schedule for the Community medium-term programme on equal opportunities for women (1986 to 1990).

---

[1] OJ L 39, 14.2.1976, p. 10.

Commission
communications

A code of practice on the implementation of equal pay for work of equal value for women and men COM(96) 336 final, 17. 7. 1996

Summary

Introduction

The principle of equal pay for men and women for work of equal value is based on Article 119 of the Treaty of Rome and on the 1975 directive relating to the application of the principle of equal pay for men and women [1].

Despite these provisions of Community law having been adopted and transposed into the legislations of the Member States 20 years ago, the differences in pay between women and men remain considerable. Indeed, information available on the manufacturing and retail trade sectors (by way of an example) shows a significant disparity between women and men's wages in all the Member States.

What is more, it is confirmed that these pay differences are even greater for non-manual than they are for manual workers, which reflects the many different types of job available and the tendency for men to occupy managerial positions and women to be secretaries, whereas in the case of manual workers, the distribution of jobs, and therefore of pay is more restricted (the calculation of the disparity of women and men's pay is based on gross average hourly pay for manual workers and on gross average monthly pay for non-manual workers).

However, it is worth noting that the average wage is calculated on a general base which includes the pay both for full- and part-time workers. The fact that the proportion of women with a part-time job is greater than that of men could partly explain why they make up a greater proportion of those on low pay.

The difference between women and men's incomes is due to many factors and in particular:

— to the vertical and horizontal segregation of jobs held by women and men (so-called female jobs are still generally less well paid),

— to the numerous sectors of the economy where mainly men work offering extra pay, working time bonuses etc, all of which widen the pay disparities between the sectors outside of the base rates,

— to the considerable differentiation in pay resulting from collective agreements linked to the recognition of skills, to the type of business and the type of industry or sector. Gender-specific segregation in employment applies to each of these divisions, increasing the potential for such differentiation,

— to the systems of collective agreements which allow salary structures to reflect the negotiating power of different groups of employees. As a result, women are generally weaker in negotiations.

In order to help lessen this difference, the Commission has decided to adopt this code of practice which follows on from its memorandum on equal pay for work of equal value, published in June 1994 [2].

The code aims to provide concrete advice for employers and collective bargaining partners at business, sectoral or intersectoral level to ensure that the principle of equality between women and men performing work of equal value is applied to all aspects of pay. In particular it aims to eliminate sexual discrimination whenever pay structures are based on job classification and evaluation systems.

The code is intended to be applied in the workplace both in the public and the private sector. Employers are encouraged to follow the recommendations in the code, adapting them to the size and the structure of their businesses. The nature of the approaches and measures set out in the code is neither exhaustive nor legally binding but provides models for action which could be taken in the area in question. The code should be read in conjunction with the memorandum, which illustrates the principle of equal pay in the light of the decisions of the Court of Justice of the European Communities.

---

[1] Directive (EEC) No 75/117 of the Council OJ L 45, 19.2.1975, p. 19.

[2] COM(94) 6 final.

Codes of practice are more widely and effectively applied when they have been conceived in close cooperation with the intended users. This is why the Commission consulted the social partners on the content and drafting of the current code. It was essential for the code to reflect, as far as possible, the approach proposed by the social partners, which was that the code should be short, its use voluntary and effective, and that it should be capable of being used during different stages of collective bargaining.

Essentially the code proposes two things:

— that negotiators at all levels, whether on the side of the employers or the unions, who are involved in the determination of pay systems, should carry out an analysis of the remuneration system and evaluate the data required to detect sexual discrimination in the pay structures so that remedies can be found,

— that a plan for follow-up should be drawn up and implemented to eliminate any sexual discrimination evident in the pay structures.

Part I — Addressees of the code

A. Businesses

The code is principally aimed at employers, regardless of whether they are from the public or private sector, because the principle of equal pay for work of equal value must in the first instance be applied by employers, who are required to pay equal wages whenever work of equal value is being carried out by male and female workers and whenever a difference in pay cannot be explained or justified other than on the basis of the worker's sex.

It is worth noting the particularly important role played by the public authorities as employers. Indeed, the full application of the principle of equal pay in the public sector would have an added value by serving as a good example.

Businesses, are of course invited, in agreement with their staff and/or their representatives, to apply the measures proposed in the code, in the manner most suited to their size and structure.

B. Partners in wage negotiation

The code targets the social partners directly. Indeed, most pay scales are the result of collective bargaining at sectoral or intersectoral level. The Court of Justice of the European Communities has also stated on a number of occasions that collective agreements must respect the principle of equal pay for the same work or work of equal value.

The task is therefore one of helping the parties in wage negotiations to remove all direct or indirect discrimination from the collective agreements concerned, thereby obtaining equal recognition for the work of women and men when the job requirements to be met are equal.

Indeed it would be desirable if at this level and subject to any necessary adjustments, the type of approach proposed could also be applied in relation to analysis of pay structures and follow-up action.

C. Individuals

Finally, the code also aims to assist women and men who believe their work is undervalued because of sexual discrimination to obtain the necessary information to resolve their problem through negotiation or, as a last resort, to bring the matter to the national courts.

*   *   *

It should be noted in this respect that the question of equal pay goes far beyond a mere study of pay structures within any one business, sector or group of sectors. It also requires action at national level not only on behalf of employers' and employees' associations but also by governments. To this end, for example, a national-level statistical apparatus allowing a survey to be carried out concerning the relative pay rates found in various branches, sectors or regions could prove to be an effective instrument in the measurement of the extent to which a worker's sex accounts for the differences established.

Part II — Study of pay structures

The study of pay structures aims to reveal any possible under-valuation of work typically carried out by women in comparison with that typically carried out by men and vice-versa. To this end the employer must determine, preferably in agreement with the staff and/or their representatives, what useful pieces of information should be gathered and then evaluate this information to see if there are signs of any procedures and practices relating to pay which are at the root of instances of discrimination.

This study should comprise three phases. First the relevant information should be collected and then it should undergo a two-stage evaluation. The first stage would be to draw up a general table showing the sex and pay of workers, and then the second stage would consist in analysing those pay-related elements identified as potentially discriminatory.

A. Relevant information

Information relevant for the purposes of the analysis should be collected across the whole of the organisation's workforce. Pay analysis within one establishment or within an individual grading or bargaining structure is not adequate as problems of sex discrimination may well arise between employees who work at the same or separate establishments, across grading structures or in different bargaining units. The focus of the information collected will vary according to the structure of the company and its pay system. Some of the information set out below will not be relevant to some organisations. It is for the organisation to determine, in conjunction with its employees, what information is relevant and necessary for the analysis.

1. *Employees*

Information about employees should be obtained from personnel and payroll records to show:

— gender

— grade

— job title

— hours of work excluding breaks

— bargaining unit or collective agreement

— required entry qualification

— other relevant qualifications

— length of service with organisation

— length of service with other relevant organisations

— basic pay

— additional payments and contractual benefits

The information should include temporary staff as well as those who are on permanent contracts and any employees who work as homeworkers/outworkers.

2. *Pay arrangements and practices*

Information about pay arrangements and practices should be obtained from the organisation's rules, handbooks and collective agreements. This will vary from organisation to organisation but may include:

— job descriptions

— grading, classification and evaluation systems

— grading/classification criteria

— pay provisions of collective agreements

— rules governing entitlement to pay and other contractual benefits

— job evaluation manual

— performance pay handbook

— rules governing the operation of bonus and incentive schemes

— piece work or contract work pay arrangements

— information on the market situation of individual jobs where relevant.

It is important that information is also obtained on pay arrangements and pay practices which follow custom and practice as well as formal rules.

B. Assessing the general information

The first stage of the assessment of the information should be the establishment of a general picture on gender and pay. An analysis may reveal that the pay system rewards employees by reference to qualifications. It may be that the qualifications rewarded do not reflect the informal qualifications which women have acquired. For example, in some Member States sewing skills might not attract a certificate but sewing machinists could not undertake the work without such skills. The definition of qualifications may need to be reviewed and in some cases expanded. Are the qualifications necessary for the jobs performed?

Where a large organisation has a complex pay structure, a clear course of action to address discrimination identified may not emerge. Therefore the wage structure should be transparent.

The general picture will provide an overview of pay arrangements and will assist in the identification of areas for priority attention. Particular aspects of the pay system will require a greater depth of analysis.

Examples of key indicators of potential sex bias are given below:

— women have lower average earnings than men with the same job title.

— women have lower average earnings than men in the same grade.

— women in female dominated unskilled jobs are paid less than the lowest male dominated unskilled job.

— jobs predominantly occupied by women are graded or evaluated lower than jobs predominantly occupied by men at similar levels of effort, skill or responsibility.

— women are paid less than men with equivalent entry qualifications and length of service.

— where separate bargaining arrangements prevail within one organisation those dominated by men receive higher pay than other bargaining groups dominated by women.

— the majority of men and women are segregated by different grading, classification and evaluation systems.

— part-time or temporary workers, who are mainly women, have lower average hourly earnings than full-time or permanent employees in the same job or grade.

— part-time or temporary workers, who are mainly women, have access to fewer pay and other contractual benefits.

— different bonus arrangements, piece rate and other 'payments-by-result' systems, apply in different areas of production affecting disproportionately one gender.

— different bonus, piece rate and other 'payment by results' calculations apply to different jobs in the same department affecting disproportionately one gender.

— different overtime rates apply in different departments affecting disproportionately one gender.

— holiday entitlements vary between jobs in the same grade affecting disproportionately one gender.

Whilst the findings above do not in themselves mean that there is unlawful sex discrimination in the pay system, they all merit further investigation. Each element in the make-up of pay or in the entitlement to pay and other contractual benefits needs to be analysed to ensure that there is an objective justification which is not affected by the sex of the workers explaining the differences in pay.

C. Particular aspects of the pay system

Practices will vary from organisation to organisation and this will affect the outcome of the analysis. Set out below are examples of practices which might prove to be discriminatory together with guidance on how to address them. However, it should be stressed that these practices are only mentioned as examples and that it is in no case implied that they are to be found in all organisations.

1. *Basic pay*

— **Women are consistently appointed at lower points on a pay scale than men are.**

Examine recruitment and promotion records to see if different treatment is objectively justifiable irrespective of sex.

Are qualifications rewarded by allowances necessary for the posts? Is the way qualifications are defined affecting women adversely?

— **Women are paid less than male predecessors in the job.**

Check if job duties and responsibilities are the same or have changed. Do the changes justify any pay reduction?

— **Women progress more slowly through incremental scales and/or seldom reach higher points.**

Check whether service pay is linked to ability to do the job rather than length of service. Where women have broken or shorter periods of service because of family responsibilities, they may be less able to meet length of service criteria.

Investigate criteria by which employees are progressed through a scale.

— **Men are paid more, by supplement or by a higher grading, because of 'recruitment and retention' problems.**

Adopt measures to deal with recruitment and retention problems e.g. existing staff could be trained and then avail of development initiatives. The pool from which staff are normally drawn could be expanded. For example clerical and non-manual staff might be considered for management training and apprenticeships through the use of positive action.

2. *Bonus/performance pay and piece rates*

— **Female and male manual workers receive the same basic pay but men have access to bonus earnings.**

Check if the differences in access to bonus can be objectively justified irrespective of sex. Do the differences in earnings reflect real differences in productivity? Investigate how access to overtime, weekend and shift working is provided.

— **Performance pay is only available to senior posts/full timers/employees covered by the appraisal system.**

Check if the coverage of the scheme and the exclusions are objectively justified.

— **Women consistently receive lower performance ratings than men.**

Review the criteria for performance rating to identify direct and indirect sex discrimination.

3. *Pay benefits*

— **A smaller percentage of women employees than men are covered by the organisation's pay benefits.**

Check the eligibility requirements for pay benefits (such as sick pay, pensions, low-interest loans, share options scheme or other allowances) to ensure there is no indirect discrimination in particular in the criteria.

4. *Part-time workers*

— **Part-time workers receive lower hourly pay rates or they are excluded from bonuses and benefits.**

Part-time workers are often excluded from pension and sick pay schemes. They may be required to work many more years than full time workers before they are eligible for training or service payments. Unless a clear and objective explanation is provided, the exclusion of part-time workers is likely to amount to sex discrimination. Check whether part-time workers are treated differently and, if so, why.

5. *Job classification, grading, evaluation and skills/competency-based systems*

Job evaluation, grading classification and skills/competency-based systems are mechanisms which are used in some Member States to determine the hierarchy or hierarchies of jobs in an organisation or group of undertakings as the basis for pay systems. The following comments are to assist those organisations which use such schemes to analyse them to check they do not inadvertently discriminate against typically female workers in particular. Pay systems based on such schemes may have been in place in organisations for many years, without any review and many incorporate features which contribute to the undervaluing of work undertaken by women.

5.1. NATURE OF THE ORGANISATION

What is the objective of the organisation? What is its nature? What services and/or products does it provide?

Asking these questions will contribute to a determination of whether the design of the scheme reflects reasonably the priorities of the organisation. It may transpire that by valuing certain elements in work the priority of the organisation is not reflected. For example, a scheme in a hospital which fails to value at all the care of patients but over-emphasises financial skills and responsibilities may require review.

5.2. TYPE OF SCHEME

Is the scheme capable of measuring the different elements in diverse work or does it rank jobs without such assessments?

Are different jobs covered by different schemes, for example one for manual and one for clerical workers, or are all jobs covered by the same scheme? In the latter case, is the system capable of evaluating evenly the work performed by different groups of employees?

Is it appropriate to the jobs covered?

Because of gender segregation in the labour market and the argument that traditional job evaluation and classification schemes are not capable of classifying inherently different work on a uniform scheme, often there has been no common yardstick for measuring typically male and female jobs. Schemes which do not cover certain types of predominantly female work obviously cannot determine whether such work may be equally demanding, albeit in different ways, as male work. The concept of equal pay for work of equal value requires the measurement of diverse work by reference to a common standard. Whilst this approach is not common, some organisations are attempting to integrate manual and clerical jobs into unified systems. If such a scheme is put in place it assists in the removal of sex bias normally associated with gender-segregated pay structures.

5.3. JOB TITLES

Are different job titles given where similar work is undertaken?

Different job titles may be given to the same or similar jobs distinguished only by the gender of the job holder e.g. storekeeper, store assistant. This may have implications for status and pay levels.

5.4. JOB CONTENT

Do the job descriptions describe all the work of the jobs and of typically female jobs in particular?

Do the job descriptions accurately describe the content of the tasks performed? In particular, is traditionally female work adequately captured? Is attention drawn to aspects of women's work which have previously gone unrecognised?

Is the work content of jobs consistently described?

Job descriptions should be constant in format irrespective of the sex of the person carrying out the occupation. There are often inconsistencies in the way male and female work is described.

5.5. FACTORS

A factor in a formal job evaluation scheme is an element of a job which is defined and measured, such as skill or mental effort. A factor may in turn be divided into sub-factors which go into greater detail under a particular heading. Jobs to be evaluated are assessed against the factors and sub-factors chosen.

Have any significant job features been omitted?

Some factors may favour one sex only. It should be ensured that factors capture both male and female work.

Factors which are more likely to be present in female jobs may not be identified at all by a scheme and therefore not valued at all, for example caring skills and responsibilites, human relations skills, organisational skills/responsibilites, manual dexterity and/or co-ordination, etc. Categorising jobs by reference to light or heavy work or weighting different factors without taking account of other elements in female as opposed to male work impacts adversely on women.

Does the job classification based on factors, or the weighting of these factors, respond to objective criteria?

Classifying work by reference to formal qualifications alone can in some instances impact adversely on women. There are skills which cannot be learned by experience alone but which benefit from formal education and qualifications. However, the qualifications or skills which many women have gained are frequently not identified as qualities to be counted positively when classifying work in the labour market. For example, nurturing, cleaning and caring skills may be assumed in certain types of work and not rewarded in pay systems. A kindergarten nurse's training may be school-based and therefore less well rewarded than typically male jobs which may be apprenticeship based.

Formal qualifications are generally rewarded but those learnt through a different process are frequently ignored. For example, experience learned in the home or by example from another worker may not be credited in the payment system. Thus the basis on which training and qualifications are rewarded may need to be reviewed.

* * *

Further to this assessment, the determination of the pay rates to be attached to the final job evaluation should reflect the relativities of actual demands of the work not 'the rate for the job' which may be influenced by traditional sex-based assumptions of worth. Therefore women should attract the pay levels enjoyed by male occupations with which their work has been found to be equivalent.

Part III — Follow-up action to target equal pay

A. Approach

Once the pay-structure study is completed, follow-up action is needed to tackle every instance of sexual discrimination detected in the pay structure. The aim of this action should be the elimination of all discrimination by applying, as soon as possible, the principle of equal pay for work of equal value. The options chosen to tackle any discrimination ascertained will depend on many factors including the size and the structure of the business as well as the nature and extent of the discrimination.

The level of collective bargaining involved will also have a considerable impact on the measures for eliminating pay discrimination. When the pay structure under consideration is the result of a collective agreement concluded at a higher level, (e.g. sectoral or national) it is at that level that action needs to be taken in cases where sexual discrimination is detected. If the agreement covers a number of very different workplaces with different proportions of women and men on the pay-roll, other studies may be needed to determine whether the problem of pay discrimination applies to all, or most, of the workplaces concerned.

This follow-up action must be evaluated in order to establish how the matter of equal pay is progressing. Whenever pay structures are subsequently adjusted a study will be needed to ensure that sex-based discrimination does not reappear. Regular reviews of pay structures are then recommended — every three years for example — to verify that the principle of equal pay for work of equal value is being respected.

B. Points which could feature in a follow-up action

The follow-up action to remedy the problems of discrimination found to exist in a given pay system could comprise:

- a merging of those jobs which are gender-specific in terms of the workers who carry them out and application of the higher rate of pay which the men receive;

- efforts to harmonise pay systems which create barriers between different types of job (e.g. office jobs and production jobs);

- a redefinition and re-evaluation of formal qualifications. For example, certain skills which women are likely to acquire in an informal manner could be taken into account and put on an equal footing with formal skills that are traditionally male (plumbing, stone and brickwork, etc.);

- a re-evaluation of the skills which traditionally are more women's than men's (e.g. manual dexterity);

- a reorganisation of work by broadening the employment categories to allow women to access typically masculine jobs where conditions are better;

- the organisation of active training measures to allow access to jobs where the other sex predominates; for example the organisation of courses allowing women to take up apprenticeships for mechanical jobs, which until now have attracted mainly men;

- an extension of the various advantages to include part-time workers.

C. Evaluation of the follow-up action

To evaluate the implications of the proposed follow-up action and to avoid perpetuating sexual discrimination, the following questions need to be asked:

- What is the effect, for each sex and the workforce as a whole, of the proposed follow-up action aimed at securing equal pay for work of equal value?

    (1) how many women are better paid as a result?

    (2) how many women see their pay blocked or remain at the same level of pay?

    (3) how many women are worse paid as a result?

    (4) how many men are less well paid as a result?

    (5) how many men see their pay blocked or remain at the same level of pay?

    (6) how many men are less well paid as a result?

    (7) what are the movements of men and women in any grading, classification, evaluation or competence system?

- What levels of pay does the follow-up action propose?

- Are groups of employees, such as part-time workers, excluded from certain procedures and conditions of employment?

- What proposals does the action plan make concerning bonuses, piece work and other pay systems based on results or output?

- Will there be a period of transition for the application of equal pay? If so, how long? Is it reasonable?

- What procedures are proposed with regard to the schedule for regular pay negotiations?

- What levels of pay and employment conditions are proposed for new staff?

It must be ensured in every case that the follow-up action brings about an improvement in pay and other work conditions and does not have the opposite effect.

Conclusion

The aim of the code is to serve as a working tool for the greatest possible number of social actors who are likely to be in a position to further the principle of equal pay for women and men for work of equal value.

This initiative should therefore be seen as part of a dynamic follow-up exercise involving management and labour plus other parties concerned at all levels capable of ensuring both a wide dissemination and an effective use of the code.

At European Union level and in the context of the fourth community action programme on equal opportunities for men and women (1996-2000), which was adopted by Council Decision 95/593/EC([1]), the will to mobilise all those who are concerned with the economic and social questions of everyday life as well as those who work in the legal sphere to focus on this problem has already been clearly expressed.

In the light of the recommendations made by the European Parliament in its report on the memorandum on equal pay for work of equal value (PE 213.161/final), adopted on 21 December 1995, the Commission in cooperation and/or jointly with the social partners and other appropriate authorities, will be able to develop further and/or support initiatives aimed at promoting such schemes as:

— campaigns to raise awareness and provide information on equal pay for work of equal value, targeting, in particular, employers, employees and/or their representatives, as well as the parties involved in collective bargaining;

— the training of experts who can study and propose practical solutions to resolve problems affecting equal pay;

— the greater involvement of women in the processes of collectively negotiated wage settlements;

— the identification, examination and exchange of best practice likely to enrich the code by providing concrete examples of the type of measures that it proposes, as well as their practical implementation.

([1]) OJ L 335, 30.12.1995, p. 37.

Incorporating equal opportunities for women and men into all community policies and activities
COM(96) 67 final, 21. 2. 1996

I. Introduction

1. The issues

Equality between men and women is now indisputably recognised as a basic principle of democracy and respect for humankind.

However, transforming it into legislation and practical reality presents a considerable challenge for societies with a long history of inequality behind them: in both industrialised and developing countries, inequalities between women and men are still apparent.

The challenge is to build a new partnership between men and women to ensure that both participate fully on an equal footing in all areas and that the benefits of progress are evenly distributed between them. Such a change requires not only progress in the field of legislation but also nothing short of a cultural transformation of individual behaviour as much as of attitudes and collective practices, and determined political action based on the broadest possible mobilisation.

The challenge facing the European Union is to build this new partnership between women and men, taking into account the historic and cultural diversity of the Member States, and drawing on this to develop a European approach to equality which is both pluralistic and humanistic and which constitutes the basis for action both in the Community and in the rest of the world.

The Union's commitment to this objective is a logical extension of the active role it played at the recent United Nations conference held in Beijing, in particular its involvement in formulating the final declaration and the action platform.

For this purpose, it is necessary to promote equality between women and men in all activities and policies at all levels. This is the principle of 'mainstreaming', a policy adopted by the Community, and attention was drawn to its crucial importance at the Beijing conference. This involves not restricting efforts to promote equality to the implementation of specific measures to help women, but mobilising all general policies and measures specifically for the purpose of achieving equality by actively and openly taking into account at the planning stage their possible effects on the respective situations of men and women (gender perspective). This means systematically examining measures and policies and taking into account such possible effects when defining and implementing them. Thus, development policies, the organisation of work, choices relating to transport or the fixing of school hours, etc. may have significant differential impacts on the situation of women and men which must therefore be duly taken into consideration in order to further promote equality between women and men.

Equal participation of women and men is a crucial factor for lasting development and symbolises the level of political maturity of societies: while democracy requires equal rights for women, this in turn guarantees democracy. Meeting this challenge could therefore be part of the European project for the twenty-first century. By firmly committing itself to take into consideration the respective priorities and needs of women and men in all its policies and measures, the Community would demonstrate its attachment to democracy and its attention to the concerns of the citizens. Furthermore, European societies would thus provide a forward-looking solution to the demographic and family changes with which they are confronted and which, given the ageing population, transform women's employment into a definite advantage for the economy which should be put to the best possible use with a view to ensuring optimum use of human resources.

2. The *acquis*

Since its creation, the Community has recognised the principle of equal pay for men and women and on this basis has developed a consistent set of legal provisions aimed at guaranteeing equal rights to employment, vocational training and, to a large extent, social protection.

In order to promote equality in practice, the Community has implemented specific action programmes since the 1980s, which, though having limited budgetary resources, have had a substantial knock-on effect. These programmes funded positive actions and pilot projects which extended the Community's field of action to the reconciliation of family and working life, women's role in the decision-making process, the participation of women in economic life and employment, etc. The Community thus promoted the creation over the years of a complex series of networks of people playing an active role in equal opportunities policy at European level but at the same time representing the cultural diversity of the Member States. It also enocuraged the work of organisations promoting equal opportunities, helping to identify good practices and, notwithstanding the conflicts between rival organisations for the promotion of women, fostered the development of possible approaches towards concerted actions to promote equal opportunities.

The Community has also continued to further the cause of women and remove inequalities between men and women through its dialogue with non-member countries, in particular through its policies on development cooperation and the promotion and protection of human rights[1]. Mainstreaming of gender issues has, in actual fact, been integrated in the Community's development cooperation policy for some years.

On the strength of the *acquis* of Community law and the experience and legitimacy gained from the programmes and networks it supported, the Community has been able to participate actively in strengthening the role of women and promoting equal opportunities at international level. It played a decisive role in the preparations which enabled the United Nations conferences in Vienna, Cairo, Copenhagen and, just recently, Beijing to go ahead. The intense interest generated by the last conference, which was put into practical effect in the pledges made on the platform, calls for Community action to be continued.

The Commission has also applied an equal opportunities policy to its staff for many years.

Community action to promote equality between women and men appears overall to be both significant and modest. Significant, in view of the narrow legal basis which gives specific competence only in matters of equal pay (Article 119 of the Treaty), and therefore the obligation in the majority of cases to obtain the unanimity of the Member States on proposals which do not strictly belong to this field. Significant, too, in view of the results obtained despite the meagre financial resources allocated specifically to the promotion of equal opportunities. But decidedly modest with regard to the size of the problem and the expectations it generates, and in view of the resources which might have been allocated for a long time now if equal opportunities had been recognised as a horizontal priority objective of Community policies. Admittedly, a large number of Community activities contribute at least indirectly to equal opportunities for women by, for example, generally promoting monetary stability, economic growth, development of employment, free movement, etc. But the positive effects of these actions on the situation of women are often not very apparent and sometimes uncertain.

The Essen, Cannes and Madrid European Councils stressed that promoting equal opportunities for women and men, together with

[1] cf. the Commission Communications on integrating gender issues in development cooperation (COM(95) 423 final of 18 September 1995) and on the external dimension of human rights policy (COM(95) 567 final of 22 November 1995).

combating unemployment, was one of the paramount tasks of the Union and its Member States. A determined effort must therefore be made to pursue and intensify the action already taken. The Commission intends to make an active contribution to the efforts required and to mobilise all Community policies towards this end. It has proposed a new equal opportunities action programme (1996-2000)[1], which should enable progress to be made in the field of legislation, the effective development of the principle of mainstreaming and the support and organisation of specific measures to promote equal opportunities. The programme was prepared on the basis of a very extensive consultation procedure and this procedure will be continued through the work of the Advisory Committee on Equal Opportunities, the composition and role of which has been modified for this purpose[2]. The Council recently adopted the Decision establishing this programme, reducing, however, the budget allocated to it in the Commission's proposals[3].

3. Mobilisation of all Community policies

Action to promote equality requires an ambitious approach which presupposes the recognition of male and female identities and the willingness to establish a balanced distribution of responsibilities between men and women. It calls for the active involvement of women but also of men and the mutual recognition of their respective responsibilities. The promotion of equality must not be confused with the simple objective of balancing the statistics: it is a question of promoting long-lasting changes in parental roles, family structures, institutional practices, the organisation of work and time, etc. and does not merely concern women, their personal development and independence, but also concerns men and the whole of society, in which it can encourage progress and be a token of democracy and pluralism. This applies not only to Europe and industrialised countries but also to developing countries.

The promotion of equality between women and men, therefore, does not simply require the implementation of positive measures targeted at women, e.g. to promote their access to education, training or employment. It also requires measures aimed at adapting the organisation of society to a fairer distribution of men's and women's roles, e.g. by adapting the organisation of work to help women as well as men reconcile family and working life; or by encouraging the development of a multitude of activities at local level to provide more flexible employment solutions, again for both men and women; or by guaranteeing the rights of fathers as much as those of mothers so that both can be expected to carry out their responsibilities and duties to the full; or by adapting social protection to incorporate the trend towards the individualisation of rights into collective responsibility, etc.

The systematic consideration of the differences between the conditions, situations and needs of women and men in all Community policies and actions: this is the basic feature of the principle of 'mainstreaming' which the Commission has adopted. This does not mean simply making Community programmes or resources more accessible to women, but rather the simultaneous mobilisation of legal instruments, financial resources and the Community's analytical and organisational capacities in order to introduce in all areas the desire to build balanced relationships between women and men. In this respect, it is necessary and important to base the policy of equality between women and men on a sound statistical analysis of the situation of women and men in the various areas of life and the changes taking place in societies.

This global, horizontal approach requires mobilisation, which is why the Commission has set up, under the auspices of its President, a Group of Commissioners responsible for stimulating the debate and ensuring that the concern for equal opportunities for women and men is built into all Community activities. An inter-departmental group has been appointed to prepare and monitor this work, and this is now taking note of initiatives planned or in progress with a view to identi-

---

[1] cf. COM(95) 381 final of 19 July 1995. Fourth medium-term Community action programme on equal opportunities for women and men (1996-2000).
[2] Commission Decision of 19 July 1995, OJ L 249, 17.10.1995.
[3] Decision of 21 December 1995.

fying possible synergies and cooperation between them.

This Communication is the outcome of that analysis and is divided into two parts:

(i) the first part presents the Community *acquis* and prospects for future action in six areas: employment and the labour market, the status of women entrepreneurs and assisting spouses in SMEs, education and training, people's rights, external relations, information; added to these six areas is the Commission's personnel policy;

(ii) the second part presents the role of the Structural Funds, which constitute the Community's main financial instrument, and which provide assistance in several of these areas.

This analysis probably does not exhaust all the measures which the Community may take to contribute to equal opportunities. However, it gives an overall picture which calls for greater consistency and complementarity between the various Community measures and which provides evidence of the inter-departmental cooperation already under way.

II. The *acquis communautaire* and prospects for future action in the field of equal opportunities

1. Employment and the labour market

Employment is one of the key areas for equal opportunities: access to employment is one of the basic elements necessary for equal opportunities for women, and job structure and conditions of work and pay are important indicators of progress — as yet insufficient — in the field of equal opportunities.

In this respect, the situation has improved, at least for the well-qualified women of the younger generations who have had greater access to the higher and intermediate categories of the labour market, particularly in the public sector, teaching and health. This trend has accentuated the disparities within the female population. However, the predominant feature of the labour market is the continuing inequality and job segregation between men and women: the proportion of women employed in administration and services has increased; likewise, the majority of insecure and part-time jobs are filled by women, which is why most jobs created during the past few years have been taken up by women.

Women's rate of participation in the labour force has increased and, on average, two out of five jobs within the European Union are now occupied by women. Women's employment situation varies widely, however, from one Member State to another, in particular with regard to the rate of labour force participation, frequency of part-time work and the unemployment rate.

The Community has been a prime mover in promoting equal employment opportunities, in particular by means of the directives enshrining the principle of equal pay and, to a large extent, equal treatment with regard to social security in European law.

The action programmes for equal opportunities implemented since 1982 have promoted studies, experiments and discussions of the policies most likely to promote equality in the field of employment, in particular through the development of positive actions, the reconciliation of family and working life, the promotion of female entrepreneurship, and local development; they have thus encouraged the implementation of pilot projects and their development into transnational networks.

The Structural Funds and, in particular, the European Social Fund have for a long time provided substantial financial support for measures promoting the training and employment of women. This contribution is dealt with in Part III of this Communication.

In addition to its activities in the context of the Structural Funds, the Commission intends to continue the efforts undertaken in two areas:

• Firstly, it is necessary to continue to construct the legal basis for equality, in particular by means of directives and/or agreements which might be concluded by the social partners on flexible working time, the burden of proof and initiatives relating to child care, home working, equal pay and the individualisation of social protection rights. It should be pointed out in this respect that an initial agreement has been concluded between the social partners under the social protocol on the reconciliation of family and working life.

- The Commission intends to rationalise and integrate its aid more effectively for studies and pilot projects relating to women entrepreneurs, reconciliation of family and working life and desegregation of the labour market. This is one of the objectives of the new equal opportunities programme which has just been adopted. Generally speaking, as far as employment is concerned, this programme is to be used as an instrument to exchange experience and encourage analysis and debate, in association with the Member States, and taking into account the discussions and measures on employment initiated after the Essen, Cannes and Madrid European Councils. An intensification of efforts to promote equal opportunities in the field of employment is one of the guidelines agreed at Madrid, and issues relating to the organisation of work, active employment policies, new sources of employment, etc., which ar the subject of these discussions and measures, are particularly relevant in this case.

2. Women entrepreneurs and assisting spouses in SMEs

Women play an important role in the administration and management of SMEs, firstly as entrepreneurs: of the 16 million SMEs in the Union (EU-12), 20-30% are managed by women; in addition, 25-35% of new businesses are created by women. Secondly, they play a role as assisting spouses to the manager: in 60-80% of SMEs, the manager's spouse carries out administrative and management duties and he/she is, with or without official status, the manager's closest associate and may even be described as a genuine co-entrepreneur; it is generally acknowledged that the greater the assisting wife's role in the

running of the company, the greater the chances of the company's survival. Moreover, in some sectors such as fisheries, the activities of each of the spouses are complementary; likewise in rural areas, where 10% of farm managers are women, farmers' wives are directly involved in the development of farm tourism and local services.

Women entrepreneurs and assisting spouses are faced with various difficulties and constraints:

— lack of business training at the time of creating the company and during its first years of existence;

— lack of recognition in economic circles, in particular with regard to accessibility of finance, and chronic lack of own capital;

— problems in reconciling family and working life;

— difficulty in obtaining access to sources of information;

— little or no recognition of the status of assisting spouse.

The Commission's enterprise policy is aimed at all sectors and all entrepreneurs, men or women, and seeks in particular to foster an environment conducive to initiative and the development of enterprises, especially SMEs, to improve their financing and to promote their integration into the single market.

There are specific measures to help women entrepreneurs and assisting spouses, though resources are limited. These include training initiatives, help in creating networks (e.g. help in creating a European association of assisting spouses), the funding of measures carried out by groups of women in the social economy field, etc. The Commission also provides financial and logistical support for the organisation of conferences dealing directly with the subject of women entrepreneurs and assisting spouses (Thessaloniki (March 1994), Paris (June 1995), Barcelona (November 1995)). There are also a number of measures included in the Structural Fund operations and, *inter alia,* in Community initiatives (Leader, LEIs, NOW, ADAPT,

SMEs) which may help women entrepreneurs and assisting spouses.

There is also Directive 86/613 on equal treatment between men and women engaged in an activity in a self-employed capacity, which, however, has had little impact on account of the mildness of the obligations it imposed.

It is intended to reinforce measures to help women in SMEs in the future, in particular by improving flexibility of work and occupational skills (including use of telematics), easier access to finance and improved access to information and advice.

Continuing its support for the conferences on women entrepreneurs and assisting spouses, the Commission is currently defining the priority measures to be included in the multi-annual action programme for SMEs (1997-2000). Several initiatives will also be taken to provide better awareness of and information on the situation of women entrepreneurs and co-entrepreneurs (which will be the subject of a special chapter in the European Observatory for SMEs' annual report) and that of assisting spouses (list of training measures). Inter-departmental cooperation will be reinforced to encourage awareness of the needs of women entrepreneurs and assisting spouses in training programmes (Leonardo) and in Structural Fund initiatives. Likewise, cooperation with the Euro-info centres at the Commission's information offices will be intensified. Finally, with regard to the above-mentioned Directive 86/613, the Commission, after consulting the partners concerned, will propose an amended Directive to provide a better solution to the problems encountered.

3. Education and training

Education and training are powerful springboards towards obtaining equal opportunities for women, even though they alone cannot guarantee occupational integration equivalent to that of men. Enhancing women's skills also enriches the pool of human resources, which is good for competitiveness and growth, and persistent unwillingness or opposition to the recognition of women's skills on the labour market and in the organisation of work and their contribution to development can be considered a waste of human resources. By paving the way towards a change in mentalities, education and training may also have a significant influence on social and professional relationships between women and men, making it possible for each to develop their respective roles, thus promoting the reconciliation of family and working life for both men and women.

The situation of women as far as education and training are concerned has improved considerably, but substantial efforts must still be made to improve women's skill levels and to facilitate not only their access to employment but also their return to work after a break in their careers. Moreover, the persistence of social and cultural models or stereotypes inherited from the past has led to an insufficient diversification of the choice of school subjects and occupations made by women and also given them less access to decision-making posts. Thus, in most cases, they abandon scientific and technical subjects, new technologies and management and give preference to traditionally female occupations (either through inclination, low self-esteem or inadequate information); sometimes these make it easier to reconcile family and working life, but render more difficult certain choices of career, access to decision-making posts or the status of entrepreneur, etc. In this context, education and training can contribute to equal opportunities by making those concerned aware of the importance of this diversification of choice, by supporting women who choose less popular career paths and those who need another chance or assistance to transform an unstable job into the first stage of an integration process and, more generally, by encouraging changes in attitudes and mentalities with regard to trades and occupations.

One of the specific tasks will also be to enhance the value of occupations taken up predominantly by women, in this case the teaching profession, given its important role in determining the future capacity for adaptation to the labour market and dealing with the key issues facing society (the environment, for example).

148

Community action in the field of vocational training comprises to a large extent substantial financial support from ESF operations, which provide funding for, *inter alia,* measures to help women. The NOW initiative has of course brought about a significant change in this area.

Community action in the field of education has supported the development of transnational projects which have sought either to raise the awareness of or train all the players involved in education (teachers, pupils or students, parents, staff involved in education) or to develop suitable educational material on equal opportunities in order to help change mentalities at an early stage, prior to entry into the labour market.

In addition, the specific programmes in the field of higher education (Erasmus, Comett, Lingua) and initial and continuing training (Eurotecnet, PETRA and FORCE) have also contributed to this objective, as has the training and mobility programme set up for researchers; however, in most cases the participation of women in these various programmes has simply reflected their participation in the labour market in general.

The Socrates (education), Leonardo (training) and Youth for Europe programmes, which were devised to consolidate and rationalise external measures in the field of exchanges and pilot projects, incorporate equal opportunities either as a specific objective (Leonardo) or as a supplementary priority for inclusion in all programme measures (Socrates, Youth for Europe). The Leonardo programme focuses particular attention on women returning to work after interrupting their careers and on fields of activity in which women are under-represented. It also incorporates activities relating to the vocational training of women carried out previously by the IRIS network. It also encourages project promoters to regard equal opportunities as an essential part of all training measures.

In addition to these programmes, various education and training measures have been or are being funded, often only on a selective basis, under various budget headings and/or in the context of funding for research activities, aid for SMEs, etc.

The concept of lifelong learning is the fundamental philosophy behind the new programmes and, more generally speaking, Community action in the fields of education and training. This philosophy involves reinforcing cooperation and complementarity between programmes in the future (Socrates and Leonardo) and between these programmes and the other Community measures incorporating an 'education and training' aspect (Structural Funds: mainstream and the ADAPT and Employment initiatives, and in particular NOW; research). The monitoring and assessment of the programmes and the preparation of a White Paper on education and training will make a significant contribution in these two areas to the overall strategy proposed by the Commission under the new equal opportunities programme.

4. Rights of persons

Recognition of the principle that the fundamental rights of women and girls are an inalienable, integral and indivisible part of universal human rights was reaffirmed at the Beijing conference.

The Community has contributed to the substantial progress made in the field of recognition of rights, and the European model of equality comprises a unique collection of knowledge, laws, institutions and practices which have conferred formal rights on women and have promoted their standing in the European Union. Information concerning these rights must be widely disseminated. In addition, improvements could be envisaged in the following specific areas:

- *Measures aimed at curbing violence against women*

With regard to measures aimed at curbing violence against women within and outside the European Union, the inclusion of the concept of gender in Community programmes should make it possible to improve and support measures such as:

(i) the organisation and financing of public awareness campaigns concerning the problems of violence against women;

(ii) medical and psychological assistance and other types of care for women who are victims of violence;

(iii) the development or creation of programmes aimed at providing training in this area for the legal and medical professions, social workers, teachers and the police.

• *Women refugees*

Following on from the Resolution of the Justice and Internal Affairs Council of 20 June 1995 on the minimum guarantees to be offered in asylum procedures within the Union, the Commission is now examining the possibility of introducing a series of measures aimed at resolving the particular problems encountered by women refugees.

With regard to women refugees outside the Union, measures should be taken to ensure their safety and integrity as effectively as possible. They should also be involved in the planning, implementation and monitoring of projects and programmes designed to help them, in order that these may best take into account their specific needs.

• *Measures against trafficking of persons*

With regard to measures against trafficking of persons, the inclusion of the concept of gender should make it possible to:

• formulate laws to prevent 'sexual tourism' and the trafficking of persons, in particular the trafficking of women in prostitution networks;

• the adoption of appropriate measures in order to develop programmes aimed at re-integrating victims of such trafficking into society (legal aid, care, cooperation with NGOs, training with a view to reintegration).

The Commission took the initiative of organising a seminar and a conference on the measures which might be taken within the Union

in order to work out an overall approach which would protect the victims of such trafficking (temporary or permanent residence permit, social and legal assistance, etc.) and tighten up measures against traffickers. Related questions, such as the status of certain categories of women particularly vulnerable to abuse or exploitation of a sexual or other nature, e.g. immigrant women with a work permit which does not allow them to change employer (case of temporary domestic staff), might also be dealt with.

• *Other related questions*

The manner in which mentalities and lifestyles have evolved has led to the diversification of family structures and histories and has increased the risk of conflict over custody of children. The difficult situations which result from this are often rendered all the more dramatic and traumatic by the fact that in this area of law there is no legal system covering questions of competence, recognition and execution of judgments in the field of family law. It is therefore proposed to extend the scope of the Brussels Convention to family matters or to draw up a new convention on this subject.

A number of problems specifically affecting non-member country nationals, in particular immigrant women resident in the Community, might also be dealt with: such problems include, for example, the free movement for a short stay of non-member country nationals lawfully resident in another Member State, on the subject of which the Commission has just presented a draft Directive to the Council (COM(95) 346 final of 12 July 1995).

The members of the family of a citizen of the Union who are non-member country nationals — normally the wife and children — obtain a secondary residence permit on reunification of the family, which means that in the event of divorce or repudiation, their right of residence ceases at the same time. For this reason, a right of residence of their own, following a reasonable period of residence, would seem to offer legal security and, where necessary, help them live independently of the person with whom they were united.

5. External relations

The Commission made an active contribution to the world conferences on the environment (Rio de Janeiro, 1992), human rights (Vienna, 1993), population (Cairo, 1994), social development (Copenhagen, 1995) and women (Beijing, 1995), the conclusions of which concern, in various respects, the promotion of women, consolidation of the means of action open to them and their autonomy.

The world conference on women held in Beijing highlighted the scale of the efforts required to promote equal opportunities. It emphasised the diversity of women's situation in the different countries, in particular the continued existence in a large part of the world of major obstacles to full economic, political and social rights for women in fields such as human rights, education and health, decision-making and access to economic resources. Moreover, it reaffirmed what had been established at Rio de Janeiro, Cairo and Copenhagen concerning the essential contribution made by women to the lasting economic and social development of society.

Considerable differences exist between men and women, particularly in developing countries, with regard to their roles, responsibilities, constraints, advantages and priorities, in both the economic and social fields. Development programmes and policies which do not take these gender issues into account are not likely to result in real benefits for women and may even place them at a disadvantage. In order to achieve real progress for women, gender issues must be taken into account systematically and are the key to obtaining lasting development for the whole of society. These are the factors underlying the principle of 'gender mainstreaming', which has for several years now been an integral part of the Community's development policies and its development cooperation conventions and agreements with the ACP countries, Asia, Latin America and the Mediterranean basin. This experience has enabled the Community to develop a range of internal instruments and measures specific to this field.

In accordance with this policy, the Community is keen to ensure that its development co-operation projects and programmes focus particular attention, right from the planning stage, on the specific needs and priorities of women and men, while ensuring an equal level of participation.

At the same time, the Community is supporting large-scale positive action programmes with a view to eliminating the major disparities between women and men in developing countries, particularly in the fields of health and education.

In addition, specific programmes such as the Democracy and LINK programmes in the context of Phare and Tacis make it possible to support initiatives of NGOs which affect women more directly.

In the future, it is intended to intensify this mainstreaming of the consideration of gender issues in all development cooperation activities in the ACP countries, Asia, Latin America and the Mediterranean basin, by applying the strategies set out in the recent communication on integrating gender issues in development cooperation.

6. Information/awareness

Putting the principle of equal opportunities into practice requires the introduction of a communication strategy comprising awareness-raising activities for the general public and information activities relating to specific programmes, which must be targeted at those concerned by the programmes in question (e.g. assisting spouses, women farmers, women entrepreneurs, etc.).

Awareness-raising activities should help to challenge certain discriminatory prejudices and stereotypes. They must be directed at both men and women, and particular attention might be focused on young people, for whom information and awareness-raising activities would consolidate or supplement educational measures. These activities must also be adapted to the cultural context of each Member State.

Up to now, the Commission's communication policies in the field of equal opportunities have been aimed principally at specific sections of the public. This is the case, for example, of some of the publications, symposia and networks funded by DG V (women in the decision-making process, women and the media, etc.), the workshop organised by DG XII on women in scientific and technical research, DG XXIII's activities to help women entrepreneurs or assisting spouses, etc. In some cases, the activity has been aimed at all women (DG X's *Women of Europe* newsletter) or at all those involved, e.g. DG XXII's awareness-raising activities in the field of equal opportunities in education and training.

This list of measures highlights the increasing number of initiatives taken to promote equal opportunities in the Commission's activities, but also the need for improved coordination between the departments concerned in order to establish a consistent, systematic and visible communication policy, adapted to the various target audiences.

A communication plan in the field of equal opportunities must therefore be developed with all the parties involved and a detailed inventory of all communication operations carried out by the various departments must be drawn up for this purpose.

Under the communication plan, an overall approach to information on equal opportunities as well as sector-by-sector implementation (employment, education/training, Structural Funds, cooperation/development, etc.) will be proposed, backed up by a proposal for an equal opportunities information programme.

The dimension of 'equality between women and men' will have to be incorporated into all communication instruments used to convey the Commission's information policy (definition of target publics, selection of subjects and form of publications, including illustrations, use of opinion analysis tools, etc.).

The 'quality' of information will have to be improved and will take into account the diversity of cultures and audiences. Communication on the subject of equality will have to be extended beyond work and the social field to all aspects of life and to sectors in which women have a particular interest: the new information technologies, biotechnologies, consumer protection and the environment, to name but a few. In the field of the environment, given women's sensitivity to improvements in the quality of life, changes in consumption patterns, etc., their opinions are listened to and they already receive assistance from DG XI via organisations and NGOs in which they are widely represented.

Equal opportunities is one of the subjects which will be developed under the 'Citizens First' initiative. This initiative is one of the three main priority actions in the field of information adopted by the Commission over the next two years.

An event targeted at the general public and held on International Women's Day on 8 March, such as the organisation of a European Women's Day on a topical subject, should raise awareness of this issue. In addition, events and meetings covered by the media on subjects relating to Community policies, programmes and activities should systematically take into account the need to address both men and women and the specific issues which concern them respectively.

Inter-institutional cooperation on the subject of equal opportunities could be encouraged by strengthening cooperation between the departments responsible for information within the Commission and the European Parliament. This cooperation might also be extended to other Community insitutions.

7. The Commission's personnel policy

The Commission has applied an equal opportunities policy to its staff for many years.

The positive action programmes have been the main instrument through which this policy has been implemented, and the second of these, covering the period 1992-96, is currently in force. This programme seeks to obtain an equal number of women in categories and functions in which they are under-represented and to promote their professional development by guaranteeing them equal opportunities for career advancement and training. The positive action programme also aims to guarantee accompanying measures and social infrastructure to enable everyone, both men and women, to reconcile their family and professional obligations.

This means that equal opportunities policy is automatically incorporated into all areas of personnel management: recruitment, careers, the planning and allocation of resources, social policy, the rights and obligations of officials. Furthermore, there is a special equal opportunities unit within the Directorate for Personnel and Administration, whose task is to coordinate the implementation of equal opportunities plans drawn up by each Directorate-General within the general framework of the positive action programme, and to make all staff aware of equal opportunities.

While equal opportunities has been recognised as a horizontal priority objective of Community policy, the institution must ensure that women have a greater role to play at all stages of the planning, negotiation and decision of policies within the various Directorates-General. For this purpose, the Commission has stressed the importance of female recruitment in its recruitment policy, both with regard to recruitment at the starting grades and with a view to appointing more women to management posts in the future. As far as starting grades in Category A are concerned, the annual organisation of general competitions for Assistant Administrators (A8) attracted almost as many female applicants as male and the success rate of women, which has also improved in recent years, made it possible for the percentage of women recruited at this grade to rise to 27 %.

Accordingly, and in the context of positive actions, the Commission adopted guidelines for the recruitment and appointment of women in 1995, when the three new Member States joined the Union. This strategy, if repeated annually, should bring about a real restoration of the balance in the years to come.

III. Structural Fund operations and equal opportunities

Structural policies constitute the main Community instrument used to correct regional imbalances and to improve employment and integration prospects. The ratio of inequality in the field of employment between economically integrated regions and regions experiencing problems is 1:10[1]. Regions experiencing problems are those whose development is lagging behind, areas of industrial redevelopment and disadvantaged urban areas, rural areas, etc. The medium-term trend in the distribution of people and activities within the Community also gives cause for concern. There is a need for corrective measures to curb the trend towards increasing urbanisation and the congestion of some regions, while interior or peripheral regions are abandoned. The situation of women is worsened in such a precarious environment.

Increasing the contribution of the Structural Funds (European Regional Development Fund, European Social Fund and European Agricultural Guidance and Guarantee Fund) to the promotion of equal opportunities is therefore of great political significance. The incorporation of equality into structural policies is, firstly, a response to the need to reduce the inequalities which exist between men and women with regard to the rate of employment, the level of training, access to the labour market and involvement in the decision-making process. But it is also part of a desire to promote lasting development, by combining job and wealth creation with quality of life and preservation of the cultural and natural heritage.

Observance of the principle of equal opportunities was introduced into the regulations governing the Structural Funds in 1993. On 22 June 1994, the Council adopted a resolution on the promotion of equal opportunities for women and men through action by the Structural Funds. However, Structural Fund operations are still relatively modest, and efforts to mobilise the partners and, above all, the national and/or regional authorities re-

---

[1] The regional unemployment rates vary from 3.4 % to 34.7 %.

sponsible for devising and implementing the programming must be continued and intensified.

1. The 1989-93 programming period

During the 1989-93 programming period, the ESF was the instrument most directly involved in promoting equal opportunities. Actions implemented as part of general measures to train and help young people and the long-term unemployed find employment made it possible in particular to improve the situation of women with regard to employment. It should be noted that 5% of ESF appropriations under Objectives 3 and 4 (i.e. ECU 380 million) were earmarked specifically for operations to help women. The other Funds (ERDF, EAGGF) have contributed in an indirect and less concentrated manner to the promotion of equality, firstly by their general support for development and, secondly, where appropriate, by funding training infrastructures or complementary social facilities.

From 1991 onwards, the segregation of the labour market and social marginalisation, of which the main victims were women, led the Commission to launch a specific initiative — NOW (new opportunities for women) — with a budget of ECU 156 million. This instrument made it possible to improve vocational training and encouraged business creation by granting direct aid. Of the numerous projects assisted under the NOW initiative (1991-94), some 300 involved the creation of small businesses and cooperatives. Some projects raise women's awareness, bring them into contact and make them more receptive to an offer of training. By way of illustration, the establishment of a 'reception-training-social' centre in a very deprived area of Oporto, fitted out — with ERDF assistance — with the modern household equipment lacking in the area, made it possible to satisfy the local community's everyday needs, while at the same time encouraging practical training, itself funded by the ESF.

The main achievement of the NOW initiative has been to decompartmentalise assistance by mobilising a wide range of operators. The innovative measures taken under this initiative

and its transnational nature, thanks to the setting up of networks for the dissemination of experience, enabled promoters to have new programmes, methodologies and infrastructures which could be used on a large scale. In the light of its success in opening up new approaches towards greater consideration of women in all the Structural Funds, the NOW initiative has been renewed and consolidated (ECU 360 million for the period 1994-99).

A number of good practices have also been observed under Community initiatives such as Leader, Interreg or pilot projects financed under innovative measures supported by the Funds. These are specific examples of coordination between promotion of the principle of equality and the overall development strategy.

The Leader I initiative (1989-93) encouraged the economic diversification of rural areas by supporting new activities organised by women, for example:

(i) in Greece a project was aimed at modernising the productive base by organising and supporting domestic industry. A women's association organised various exhibition sites and managed a centre for domestic industry and handicrafts. The project, which was launched in 1990, enabled women in the region to be given continuing training in the manufacture of local quality products and craft objects.

(ii) in the United Kingdom, target groups (20 young unemployed people, 10 managers made redundant and some 15 women wishing to start up a business at home) benefited from start-up aid through the financing of feasibility studies, marketing and promotion costs, further training courses and training in local services.

Under the multi-fund transborder cooperation programme (Community initiative Interreg I) between France and Spain, some 30 women with an average age of 38 from a region affected by a high rate of unemployment because of the decline in the textile industry were helped in their career plans (creation of activity or search for a job) through training measures, training courses in the neighbouring country and the setting up of partnerships for complementary projects.

The ERDF pilot projects (Article 10) also supported measures aimed at improving back-up structures for women which would facilitate their occupational or social reintegration. The issue looked at in most detail was the improvement of the quality of life.

For example, in the United Kingdom, under a scheme to regenerate inner-city areas a multi-purpose community centre providing the equipment necessary for the regeneration programme was funded. The centre includes a family department offering a full range of services, including an original type of crèche which enables the occupational reintegration of the very large number of young mothers.

2. The 1994-99 programming period

During the present programming period (1994-99), the promotion of equal opportunities is a priority running through all the activities receiving Structural Fund assistance, with a determined effort being made to obtain greater coordination.

The promotion of equal opportunities is referred to in all ESF programming documents, especially those of Objective 3, as a priority which should apply across the board to all general measures to be supported. In a number of Member States, these programming documents also refer to a specific set of actions aimed at promoting equal opportunities (within Objective 3 or within the human resources component of Objective 1) and are intended to complement the horizontal approach adopted.

The introduction of the concept of pathways to integration as a result of the experience gained under the NOW initiative, and the relaxation of the criteria for programme eligibility, have made it possible to formulate 'packages' of personalised measures aimed at integration or reintegration into the labour market. Thus, in the field of education and training, the ERDF and the Social Fund may provide coordinated and complementary assistance, the ERDF financing the equipment

and installations and the Social Fund the operating costs.

Combined operations by the ESF, ERDF and EAGGF also help in carrying out measures and providing facilities which make it possible for women to reconcile their working and family life better (crèches, kindergartens, after-school activities, adaptation of transport in sparsely-populated areas, etc.). Measures which are directly linked to the provision of infrastructure for business areas and the creation or maintaining of jobs may be of direct benefit to women entrepreneurs and assisting spouses, as well as to the female employees of the enterprises supported. Generally speaking, operations relating to the adaptation of production activities, local development and improvement of the quality of life do not concern solely women but may have a more direct impact on promoting equality on account of their proximity effects.

The Community initiatives (such as ADAPT, URBAN I, Leader II, Interreg II) also reflect the political impetus given to equal opportunities.

Thus, in a French town, the ideas generated by the URBAN initiative about care facilities for young children led to the creation of a centre intended not only to cater for children but above all to help parents play their full part in bringing up children in an unstructured environment. In the future, European funding will enable one-parent families on a very low income to have access to jobs by creating care facilities adapted to vocational training opportunities (day-care centres with extended hours, more family crèches, etc.).

As in other fields, the Community added value is generated by bringing the various project sponsors together. The networks which initiatives such as NOW or Leader [1] have at their disposal constitute a prime means of exchanging practices and transferring experiences and methodologies.

---

[1] Leader II (94/C 180/12): 'The present network must also expand its activities, in particular by establishing a methodological instrument, the European Observatory of Rural Innovation and Development, whose role will be to identify, specify, validate and facilitate the transfer of innovations implemented in rural environments'.

Through the support given to these various measures and the strengthening of Community initiatives, the Funds facilitate the identification and dissemination of good practices and help to boost cooperation and integration under the new Equal Opportunities Programme (1996-2000).

3. Outlook

Of the proposals aimed at making sure that greater account is taken of equal opportunities, it is planned first of all to take advantage of the current programming, which means in particular that the monitoring committees will have to be alerted, in conjunction with evaluation measures.

Thought will have to be given to the indicators and ways of measuring the extent to which the principle of equal opportunities will be taken into account in the programming. Basic indicators will have to be established for certain types of measures with positive connotations for equal opportunities in order to be able subsequently to define pertinent project selection criteria for the programme monitoring committees. To this end, a horizontal evaluation study will be able to shed light on the way in which this aspect is really applied by the Structural Funds.

The production of basic regional statistics (availability of social infrastructure, breakdown of long-term unemployed by sex, female activity rates, proportion of women by socio-professional category, etc.) is also an essential prerequisite for measuring trends.

Methodological guidelines will be drawn up for the monitoring committees by several Commission departments working together.

The efforts to achieve synergies in the current programming period imply greater coordination of multi-fund operations for the launching, financing and exploitation of the results of pilot projects linked directly to the promotion of equal opportunities (Article 10 ERDF, Article 6 ESF, Article 8 EAGGF-Guidance). In this connection, special attention will be paid to measures to assist women wishing to set up their own business, along the lines of the awareness-raising operations already

carried out for the European business and innovation centres and the Euroleader programme.

Flexible programming affords scope for redirecting the multiannual programmes already adopted (1994-99 for Objective 1 and Objective 5b, 1995-99 for Objective 6, 1994-96 for Objective 2). This flexibility must be used to strengthen measures which are recognised as being effective and to explore new avenues of assistance. When the reserve for Community initiatives was allocated on 4 October 1995, the Commission decided in principle to place particular emphasis on equal opportunities in URBAN II and to give a boost of ECU 100 million to the NOW initiative.

Generally speaking, the Structural Funds may make an effective contribution towards implementing the Union's and its Member States' priorities of combating unemployment and promoting equal opportunities for women and men. In this context and in accordance with the guidelines agreed by the European Council, they may in particular encourage the search for more employment-intensive growth and the optimum use of human resources.

In order to alleviate some of the constraints which primarily affect women, the Structural Funds can be used as a matter of priority for the development of infrastructures and services for the care of dependants or for investment by enterprises to assist, through new organisation of work, the creation of jobs and reconciliation with family life.

The Funds also have to contribute to the economic and social integration of urban and rural populations that are becoming marginalised. Combating the rapid marginalisation of women who are disadvantaged and/or live in sensitive areas requires a concerted effort to reconstitute social links: for example, through the creation of social centres (multipurpose halls for sport, entertainment, distance learning, etc.) or the financing of teaching tools and business-creation support services.

These guidelines complement those relating to the promotion of new sources of employment, the adaptation of the organisation of work and skills and support for regional development and local initiatives.

A European seminar aimed at promoting equal opportunities in Structural Fund assistance will be held in Brussels on 7 and 8 March 1996, in particular to mobilise the national and regional authorities responsible for implementing the programmes and to derive maximum benefit from the efforts made. Other events are also planned, such as the organisation of exhibitions and conferences on innovation and local development for women as part of the Luleå (Sweden) Europartnership in June 1996. Lastly, promotional booklets illustrating and encouraging good practices will be produced.

IV. Conclusion

This communication is one stage in a process that must be continued in order to give more concrete expression to the principle of mainstreaming than in the past. In fact, assessing the ways in which equality between women and men has been taken into account up to now in Community policies gives rise to a series of guidelines and proposals which must now be implemented.

Without doubt, there is still a lot to be done to ensure that promotion of equality between women and men actually becomes a strategic objective fully integrated into all Community policies and that the male/female dimension is taken into consideration in the planning and implementation of those policies (gender perspective). It is quite clear above all that the progressive implementation of these guidelines calls for a significant increase in cooperation within the Commission's departments and strengthening of the partnership with the Member States and the various players and organisations concerned.

The very fact that this communication has been produced, at the instigation of the Group of Commissioners on Equal Opportunities, is evidence of the efforts that have been made within the Commission. Such efforts reflect a political commitment and a desire to give a significant impetus to Community action,

thereby supporting the efforts undertaken at all levels to promote equality between women and men.

Various measures and initiatives should in the next few months give practical effect to the cooperative efforts undertaken. 1996 will see the implementation of initiatives as a follow-up to the Beijing conference. It will also be the year of introduction of the new equal opportunities programme recently adopted by the Council, the official launch of which will give rise to a major conference in autumn 1996. Structural Fund assistance should also be confirmed, and the European seminar to be held on 7 and 8 March 1996 will provide a forum for discussion with the Member States and the other players involved. Cooperation with the social partners will continue and attention should be drawn in this connection to the fact that they have just reached an initial collective agreement under the protocol on social policy on reconciling family and working life.

1996 should lead to substantial progress in implementing the principle of mainstreaming in all Community policies, in particular in each of the fields dealt with in the second part of this communication. For this purpose, it will be necessary to take measures to continuously monitor and evaluate the action undertaken. The inter-departmental group on equal opportunities is to contribute to this, relying, where necessary, on apropriate expert reports. It will be necessary to scrutinise policies more carefully from the point of view of equality and, therefore, in order to manage, identify and evaluate their effects, to establish suitable analytical indicators and procedures. Such a systematic evaluation will make it possible to confirm that consideration of equality between women and men in the proposed measures and, by extension, in all Community policies is being practically and effectively implemented. This will be the subject of one of the chapters of the report on equal opportunities which the Commission now intends to publish each year and which will present the policies and measures implemented in the Member States as well as action taken at Community level.

European Commission

Equal opportunities for women and men
European Community acts

Luxembourg: Office for Official Publications of the European Communities

1999 — 157 pp. — 21 × 29.7 cm

ISBN 92-827-7665-4

Price (excluding VAT) in Luxembourg: EUR 15